Leave the Dirt in the Field

Mississippi, The Deception of Innocence

By
Warren Smith
2021

Copyright © 2021 by Warren Smith

All rights reserved. This book or any portion thereof may not be reproduced or used in any manner whatsoever without the express written permission of the publisher except for the use of brief quotations in a book review or scholarly journal.

First Printing: 2021
ISBN: 978-1-7379629-5-3

Ordering Information:

Special discounts are available on quantity purchases by corporations, associations, educators, and others. For details, contact the publisher at the above-listed address.

U.S. trade bookstores and wholesalers:

Please contact: *wjsmithservices@gmail.com*

DEDICATION

Growing up in the Mississippi Delta led me to believe the world was full of good and wholesome people. Once I left the sheltered life my mother and father created, I jumped into the real world. I am humbled and grateful that the realities of Mississippi life were so well hidden from me. Experiencing a wonderful upbringing in the little town of Inverness, Mississippi—was a gift from my parents. For this reason, I dedicate this book to my mother, Helen Smith, who kept me on the better side of town while struggling to survive. She worked in the white man's houses, and the cotton fields, "making ends meet" for herself. She always knew how much I appreciated her struggle to keep me focused.

ACKNOWLEDGEMENTS

Around thirty-five years ago, I served in the United States Army, I was at my best physical & mental conditioning. I ran 40-50 miles a week, did hundreds of pushups, sit-ups, and jumping jacks to stay fit. I had finally realized that my protection came from God and any glory was all because of Him. I possessed the knowledge and wisdom to be all that I wanted to be. It was then when I decided to record my journey. I wrote by the sentences; I wrote by the paragraph until my story started to develop on paper. My story is the result of a life fighting the systems of oppression and racism. Every job I held; Boeing and the Department of Veterans Affairs included, resulted in racial discrimination.

Despite the drawbacks, I excelled in leadership. The money moves I made taught me there were experiences and life outside of Mississippi. I thank the Army for all the special assignments. I am thankful to my father, George Reed, for preparing me for life. God guided me through the good and the bad.

I want to thank my brothers Theodore and Wesley for putting up with my devious youth. I want to thank my sisters Joyce and Tenia for never faltering in motivating me.

TABLE OF CONTENTS

DEDICATION	iv
ACKNOWLEDGEMENTS	v
CLEANING UP MY LIFE: A BETTER WAY TO BE CLEAN	7
WHAT MAKES THEM AFRAID OF US?	8
WHAT YOU KNOW CAN HURT YOU	14
HOME: WHERE YOU POWER UP TO CONFRONT THE WORLD	19
THE MISSISSIPPI DELTA	25
MAKE BLACK PEOPLE INVISIBLE AGAIN	34
THE BLUES IS ALRIGHT	38
NATIVE BLACK AMERICANS MATTER	45
COTTON, MORE IMPORTANT THAN PEOPLE	50
THE SEPARATE BUT EQUAL DOCTRINE	55
THE FAMILY	64
HOW WHITE PRIVILEGE CHANGED US	95
DECISION TO JOIN THE MILITARY	132
FIRST BUSINESS	152
BIBLIOGRAPHY	154
ABOUT THE AUTHOR	155

CLEANING UP MY LIFE: A BETTER WAY TO BE CLEAN

I chose to write about personal hygiene because there are many men unaware of how to clean the body. As a man, there are several ways to present yourself. I cut my hair, not only on my head but in my private areas too. A close shave of the head along with a trim of the armpits, neck, chest, stomach, buttocks, and around the manhood—leaves a fella with an all-around sense of cleanliness. Sometimes we forget that our hair continues to grow—all over—and remember if you cut the hair on your head, you should cut the hair in other places!

When I bathe, I usually use the shower. Start with two face towels, one for the face and the other for everything else. Wash the face with the face towel, scrubbing around the eyes; scrub the nose, the ears, the jaws, and the neck all the way around.

Secondly, begin lathering your hair with some quality shampoo, and don't forget the beard if you have one. Do this at least twice a week. Upon completion, fully ring out the face towel and put it away. With the second towel clean both arms, the torso, the privates, down the legs and onto the feet, and then between each toe. Finally, take a complete rinse and step out of the shower. Begin drying off the head and face, down the arms, and so on. Top off a good clean body with some name-brand cologne.

It is very important to dry between each toe after a bath or shower. According to the Toe Bro, a show on the Discovery Channel, one must clean out the crud and moisture between the toes. It is the best way to combat athletes' feet and fungi. Trimming the toenails, fingernails, and cuticles is just part of good hygiene. For men, there is nothing wrong with getting a pedicure once a month. Scraping that dead skin off your feet will make your significant other very happy. The feet are the most important part of the body; nothing is arguably worse than foot pain. Learn how your toenails grow and keep them from becoming ingrown.

WHAT MAKES THEM AFRAID OF US?

The Declaration of Independence states, *"We hold these truths to be self-evident, that **all men are created equal**, that they are endowed by their Creator with certain unalienable Rights, that among these are Life, Liberty and the pursuit of Happiness."*

Blacks were still slaves; the Declaration's ratification on July 4, 1776, did not apply yet. The Emancipation Proclamation's enactment years later in January 1863 did not exactly "free" the slaves. So, this tells me that "All Men Are Created Equal" pertained to white men only. *The Souls of Blackfolk* had little to no claim in the fight for owning the promises in these two great documents. Even as the Colored 54th Regiment was freeing slaves in the South, our stakes in America needed something more. A purchase by blood and outright victory on the battlefield would still not be enough in the years to come. Our ancestors had no stake in Amerikkka, so Black people were not fully considered in these equations.

The white man left Europe and landed in North America in Roanoke in 1585, then on the *Mayflower* in 1620. The immigrants found they were not ready for the New World. They suffered mightily in Jamestown until they were able to befriend Native Americans. After many betrayals and battles, the Native Americans became uncomfortable; Europeans and later Americans stabbed them in the back by taking land, breaking treaties, and making enemies for life. Everywhere the white man has landed on the planet earth; they bribed their way in, enslaved the natives, and prospered on the backs of their labor. This imperialist strategy has worked for hundreds of years from the Conference of Berlin in 1885 to now, especially in the Americas.

Let's "Make America Great Again" seems to be the momentum in the air these days. What exactly does that mean? It means there is a gray area existing in the slogan, it means let's go back to slavery times, back to a time where we could hang a Black Man and get away with it. Let's go back to a time when the Black man had nothing but labor for a white man. Be real with it, our presidency appeals to the rednecks and bigots in Amerikkka. Any time there was an opportunity for Americans to prosper, the Black man has always been left out of the race.

The Black American is the youngest species of human beings on the planet earth whose inalienable rights have been long denied. The white man has tried to get rid of us like roaches; it has not happened but they never stop coming after us. They use the police to kill us, the army to intimidate us, city services to crutch us, the Black woman to go against us, and the government to solidify their dirty deeds.

Who are we to be such a feared race of people? What made the white man so angry and so afraid of our Black race? Why has he, the white man, tried to keep us in bondage? When will the Black man be free of all the unfulfilled promises? Where in America, can we be accepted and respected while just being Black?

Black people are allegedly guilty for: Driving while Black, Walking while Black, Living while Black, Fishing while Black, Flying while Black, Eating while Black, Talking while Black, Hunting while Black, Shopping while Black, Sick while Black, Whistling while Black, Having money while Black, Sitting at the counter while Black, Bidding on a Contract while Black, Owning a Business while Black, Owning a gun while Black, Educated while Black and being a Father while Black! Black people are guilty of breathing the air in America; nothing is in our favor, not even Black history month.

As one learns about the documented people of the world, it becomes commonplace that Black people are the only race, in white America's eyes, to not be deserving of any form of the American dream. We always see documented white folk's heritage going back century after century stacking that old money for future generations. From World War I and II to the Korean War, Black Americans served America with valor and have yet to be recognized for their accomplishments to keep America a superpower. The Black race proved themselves in wars and in societies to be worthy of the American Dream.

Coming home from wars, Black military men and women still were made to take a back seat in America. We were expected to sit down and shut up all the time; when we did stand up, like Huey P. Newton and the Black Panthers by doing for ourselves; the federal government deployed the Central Intelligence Agency (CIA) and the Federal Bureau of Investigation (FBI) agents to shut it down. Government agencies planted drugs, guns, and lying snitches in our communities.

We can see Mexican heritage going back for centuries; I asked a Mexican the other day, "how far back can he trace his family's heritage? He replied, about three hundred years and 1000 acres that we still have in the family. We, as Black Americans, cannot imagine what having or leaving a documented ancestor would be like. When I see other races celebrating the heritage and the history of their family tree, I solidify my thoughts that the Black American is the youngest species of human beings on the planet Earth.

To place this in perspective, we are again reminded of our infant nature to the world. How do we view newborn babies? We view them as needing to learn how to grow positively. We still make comments such as "I'm going to the crib" or "hey baby let's go see a movie." Why do Black people call a house a crib or our spouses "baby?" Let us ask Google, Google looks at the term "crib" as a safe place. Maybe it is because a home is a safe place and we use the word in this vernacular because it makes us feel safe in Amerikkka.

Cultural Conditioning is what we have done to the incoming generations of Black men. Blacks are stigmatized as not being the desirable race of people to flourish in America. We have never been on the receiving end of goodness; for instance, the land grant acts of the 1890s. Nineteen universities received land to build Historically Black Colleges and Universities (HBCU) thus beginning the HBCU's in the Americas; they are Alabama A&M, Alcorn State University, Central State University, Delaware State University,

Florida A&M, Fort Valley State University, Kentucky State University, Langston University, Lincoln University, North Carolina A&T State University, Prairie View A&M University, South Carolina State University, Southern University, Tennessee State University, Tuskegee University, University of Arkansas Pine Bluff, University of Maryland Eastern Shore, Virginia State University and West Virginia State University[1].

So, what about the forty acres and a mule? Forty Acres and a Mule refer to the promise made to former agrarian Slaves in the United States. On January 16, 1865, Union Army General William Sherman and the Freedmen's Bureau Act, granted hundreds of Black families forty-acre plots of Federal Government-held land. This land had been confiscated from the southern whites as a result of the Civil War. After the assignation of President Lincoln, the appointed President Johnson, immediately ordered the land returned to its former white owners, and the Black families were made to sign labor contracts as sharecroppers for the white owners of the same land.

Again, America or shall I say the greedy white people in charge of America, abused their governmental powers to strip Blacks from a foothold in America. Blacks have grown tired of doing impossible things for the ungrateful. Step after step we have taken to become equal or better citizens, listening to what they are saying! I am not asking to be better, but just to be treated as an American citizen. One might say, equal to what? Equal to an American citizen without prejudice!

I have often tried to be very cognizant of identifying upfront, the Blackness of who I am and what I am. Each time an episode has led to the same results, we as Black people are trying not too strongly to identify who we are while other races tend to hurry to let us know what we are. They do this by oh, is that your car or a rental? As if we are not supposed to have a nice car or nice things.

---

[1] https://nifa.usda.gov/program/1890-land-grant-institutions-programs

I believe the word Black should not only be in the title of everything we stand for, but the word "Black" needs magnifying every step of the way; let people know it is the Blackness in us pushing to change the image formed of our people. It is the Black people striving to do community service and charity events, it is the Black American making the world a better place for all races.

We were brought here as slaves to be an asset to the white plantation owners. Once we were freed, we became a liability to the same white folks. As a liability, we had to be eliminated; thus came the Jim Crow laws, the KKK, lynching, and killing anyone with dark skin. Lastly, just for this answer, it is who we are, leading the push to rehabilitate Black formerly incarcerated people (FIP); it is us trying to get the veteran better ratings with the Department of Veteran Affairs.

We must understand that we are Black and American, whether someone likes it or not. There is no getting around it, away from it, or over it. This is why and how they are going to support our cause, being Black should not matter but our Black lives should not be valued as animals in America.

Each word of the thirteenth amendment is written to equalize the Black Man—failed us. *"Neither slavery nor involuntary servitude, except as a punishment for crime whereof the party shall have been duly convicted, shall exist within the United States, or any place subject to their jurisdiction."* So, what does the white man do? He increased the conviction rate of Blacks giving them longer sentences than a white man for the same crime. Blacks are locked up for any and everything and kept incarcerated because the bail money cannot be paid. The Black man does not have bail money because he does not have a job, he does not have a job because there are no industries in his neighborhood, if there were, no one will hire him in a job that pays decent wages to support his family.

The cycle of "lock up the Black Man" continues to this day! Which makes us again; hoodwinked and bamboozled about what is made equal or better for the Black man in white America. Our race of people is sick and tired of losing this fight against bettering the

Black race. It is not the white man holding us back now; it is the Black man falling deeper into the traps set for our race of people. We are so angry at what the white man has done to our ancestors and us, we just do not know what to do next.

Each time we see a Black man moving up the corporate ladder, we call him an Uncle Tom; they see him as meeting the quota. If it is a woman, then they have met two quotas, Black and female. We look at the Black man who made it in white America and offer no logic for understanding how he played the white man to get there. No matter how hard we try to get along, there is always something wrong with a Black-on-Black approach.

Take a look at the major Black players in the country; they are almost always alone on a mission to get rich. If they had a partner, they were dismissed when the money came in. Look at Jay-Z, released all ties to any associates including Kanye West. In America, Black people are always trying to get ahead by proving themselves to the white man. They think the only way Black people can succeed is to act white; learn the white way and hang with the white boys.

We are champions; we serve a greater purpose than we portray ourselves to be. We refuse to be in a situation where we can never win, yet we work with them, the white man, to build up their empire. The United States of America is a place where no matter how good one gets, not being white is a curse. Nothing here is in place to equalize the Black Man. Once a law is passed to help, another law is passed to tear you down. They have done this for centuries; when the slaves were freed, the KKK increased its membership by tenfold. This was to intimidate, raise fear, and punish the Blacks who just wanted to be free.

WHAT YOU KNOW CAN HURT YOU

Knowledge and Wisdom

Knowledge is having the facts and wisdom is applying the facts. Without wisdom, knowledge is useless. Do your wise actions measure up to your level of knowledge? You trained your kid, but the world can eat them up. Never sacrifice your coolness for someone's foolishness. It is better to be known for what you do than to be known for who you are.

There is no constitutional right to education beyond getting a high school diploma. Only motivated individuals pursue higher levels of education because they have the determination to do so. This concept is true for anything; overachievers succeed because they are highly motivated.

Justice System Inequality

Plessy v. Ferguson was a landmark Supreme Court decision that occurred in 1896. The court ruled in favor of racial segregation, as long as the separate facilities had equal provisions for whites and Blacks. This case reaffirmed that Jim Crow laws would have a place in American society.

Within the laws of justice, judges intend on sentencing Black men with twice the charges that they would give a white man for the same offense. The prison population is set up for extreme profits. Blacks flooded into the system and could never escape it. This system guarantees the inmates' availability to work plantations in the south. We never receive a warning citation from the police. Instead, they push us to the prison gates. The movie *Just Mercy* is a recent prime example of an innocent Black man getting railroaded into prosecution when the evidence and credible witnesses cleared him of any wrongdoing.

Edward Richardson—a white plantation owner during the Civil War—was perhaps Mississippi's greatest benefactor from prison labor. Richardson was the first to receive a contract from the state for prison labor. The state of Mississippi paid eighteen thousand dollars a year for the care of prisoners that he signed out of Parchment Prison to work on his plantation. The profits from the prison contracts helped Richardson regain his wealth.

Yes sir, Jim Crow exists in all aspects of Black lives! So here we are again, just released from slavery and now going to prison because the white man would not give us work. They were the only ones with industry, retail, and the capacity to give a freed slave a job. We wanted to work, and we will work for our lives if given the chance.

They devised many methods to keep us in bondage. The prison system is just another way for the rich to get free labor. Who is the lazy one? It sure isn't the Black man; Black men in US History have started work as early as five years old in enslaved times and never stop working until death. The real lazy one has never been the Black man!

Walk Tall in Your Blackness

Love thyself enough to take up guns in your defense. Love thy family enough to protect them. Love thy ethnicity enough to fight for the right to be valued.

One shall stand for righteousness in front of all people and each other. One shall defend another against disrespect as vehemently as they would defend themselves.

These beliefs, values, and ethics create a moral dilemma in our lives that demands change and homage to the presence in which we stand. Understand that this is an oath that you take without any mental reservation or moral hesitation. It's an agreement to stand, even if alone, for the belief hereof. We shall also defend who we are.

Kaepernick Kneeling

Ask Colin Kaepernick about the consequences of standing or kneeling for a cause. This man was an up-and-coming quarterback for the San Francisco 49ers and the National Football League

(NFL). When the league turned its back on him, a rule came about that banned kneeling during the national anthem. Only a few of the Blacks, who make up eighty percent of the NFL, kneeled with him. How awful! During this controversy, many Black NFL players chose to stay in the locker room during the anthem instead of kneeling on the field.

Robert, a friend of mine, recently spoke about loyalty; one would think that in the NFL, Black players would be loyal to each other and stand together. In this case, the players did not, they left Kaepernick kneeling alone. Robert also said he only goes to one bar, to work, and back home. He is loyal to these places because they provide him comfort. Unlike the team members of Kaepernick, Robert is a loyal friend.

Religion

God is the invisible source of omniscient and omnipresent power. It is difficult to believe we can navigate our lives without having help from a supreme being. So that I'm not misunderstood, I'll preface this claim by clarifying that I strongly believe in God and that He does exist in my life. However, everything, and I mean everything, ever told, preached, or taught, about Him is most likely a lie.

The movie *Car Wash* said it best, "You got to believe in something, why not believe in me?"

This depiction of a church service is a recollection of my experience watching the pulpit. Let's evaluate a typical Black church service. The church service opens with a song from the choir, the worship leader is next; his job is to excite the congregation and have the people ready to receive the pastor. The pastor walks to the podium and starts to speak. The tone of his voice is soft and slow. He may read a scripture or two from the Bible and expound on the topic from there. As he further explains the passages, he starts to elevate his voice with a growl or a rumble. The congregation encourages the pastor by saying things like, "Preach Pastor!" "Well..." And, "Yes Sir!"

Now, with the pastor reaching a crescendo, he is belting out common verses. He jumps up, spins around, and lands on his feet. Now the church band is at a frenzied pitch and the people are shouting!

At the end of the day, when everyone has left the church, they say things like "Pastor sure did preach a good sermon today! Oh yeah, what did he say? I don't know but it sure was a good show."

A good show, come on now! Is the church entertainment or what? Ask yourself this question, what do I leave behind or leave with when I leave the church? Man has force-fed religiously misleading information to the African diaspora in the Americas for generations.

Think about it, what religion did our ancestors practice before being stolen from Africa? If the teachings of the Bible are true, then how could there be so many versions of it? Why do millions of churches park themselves on the corner of our poorest neighborhoods and promise the path to salvation? I am writing this, not because I am a non-believer, but because I seek the truth from the people of the world and the United States.

Money, power, and politics rule everything in Amerikkka! The words of the Bible were written by people with power who felt the need to interpret the meaning for themselves. There are twelve major religions in the world, some of which use the Bible as a guide.

The twelve major religions and their followers:
1) Christianity, with 2.4 billion followers (they killed you in the New World if you did not follow)
2) Islam, with 1.2 billion followers
3) Catholics, with 1.1 billion (with a passion for abusing young boys)
4) Hinduism, with 828 million
5) Agnosticism, with 639 million
6) Buddhism, with 267 million
7) Atheism, with 150 million
8) Anglicanism, 85 million

9) Sikhism, with 23 million
10) Seven Day Adventist, with 16 million
11) Latter-Day Saints, with 15 million
12) Judaism, with 14 million[2]

    The thirst for power runs rampant in religious circles, even though there are many other ways to gain it. The leaders of the church mislead and misdirect the people, who are being hoodwinked and lied to every Sunday. Many preachers were once incarcerated people. They are former drug dealers, pimps, and hoes who went straight and appealed to the women flock. These are egotistical, greedy bastards who take advantage of the people who just want to find their way to God.

    Back in the day—when it was fun—we only went to church service every fourth Sunday to hear the preacher. Now, many preachers do two or three services on Sunday. It is a crazy scene: preachers scramble to hustle people out of their money, and the people are gullible enough to give it to them. A lot of preachers lie so that they can maximize monetary income. They make more by holding multiple services and passing multiple collection plates. The church is all about the power: financial power, positional power, political power, people power, Black power, white power, and the power of love. Don't forget Restoration Power, which is the most important power to me.

---

[2]*Newsmax.* 12 Most Popular World Religions. R. Grigonis, May 2014.

HOME: WHERE YOU POWER UP TO CONFRONT THE WORLD

When your car is low on gas, you go to the gas station. When your phone charge is low, you plug it into a power source. When your belly is empty, you find something to fill it. When you spend eight hours at a job, two hours in traffic and someone takes your parking spot at the grocery store, you can't wait to get home. Restoration power is that human refill you get when you make it home. When you are home, you can relax and feel 100% safe. You can shower, have dinner, watch a movie and fall asleep. Everyone can't obtain restoration power so when God sees favor in you, he will grant you restoration power.

The child, the man, and the woman need to understand this to cope with the struggle for power in the world. Most people do not want to face the reality of everyday life, they let themselves go and become a recluse. Why is everything promised by God "just around the next corner?" To get around that corner, I need to be sheep-like and follow a lie told to the people by preachers? Even then, I still may not get around that corner.

The preacher is a joke, nothing like the preachers of old. I want to tell a story that no one knows except Tenia, my middle sister. It was 1972 during the summer; I never understood why the pastor came around the house on Sundays. This particular Sunday he was at my house; we were living on Quick Circle. Reverend Brisby of New Hope Missionary Baptist Church in Inverness was in my living room sitting on my couch. In his nice suit, he looked like Dapper Dan. He was chilling on the couch and I would peek my head in the living room where he and Muddear were sitting. I assumed I was making a lot of noise in the house because when I came back by, I found the living room door closed. I kept on playing in the house until, all of a sudden, I wanted to go outside. I popped the living room door open to ask Muddear if I could go outside.

What I saw sent me into shock. I left the house running from Quick Circle and didn't stop until I got to the back part of South Gate, where Tenia was over at Bessie Lockhart's house. The reverend had his pants down, and they were both on the floor. When I opened the door, they looked up at me and I looked back at them.

All Muddear could say was, "Boy, close that door!" So, I closed it and ran all the way to South Gate. I told Tenia, and she couldn't believe it! We walked back home in the same state of shock, never uttering a word about the incident from that day until now.

That is why I say, these guys who call themselves preachers, are hypocrites to the core and the bank. They want power over women and money. There are many, many churches in the Black communities all across the country. Preachers go after the most vulnerable forms of power there is; positional power, political power, and power over the people.

The authority the preacher abuses most is guilt. He starts by speaking in three or four-word phrases and then elevating one of the words to see how the crowd reacts. He keeps a few powerful words available so he can throw them out to take the congregation up another notch. Before you know it, he is yelling, huffing, and puffing and that is what the people came there for.

At the end of the show, the congregation says, "That preacher sure can preach!" If asked what was the Word, very few could tell you because they went for the show.

When I was in boot camp back in 1977, God was trying to tell me something. The drill sergeant told me to run! Run as fast as I can to get around that corner which was about 100 yards away. I ran as fast and hard as I could to get around that corner. Do you know how one stretches out to be the winner of a relay race? I would stretch for that last step to get around that corner, never making it. Before I knew it, the drill sergeant blew his whistle. When he blew it, I had to turn around and run back to him.

Maybe then, God was trying to let me know something.

When people start to believe in what they have and not what they wish they had, it creates power. When people start to replenish and restore rather than tear down and drain, it creates power. When people start to accept who they are and how God intends to move them, then they can become powerful. The home is the cornerstone that is always just around the corner. Create the home that restores the power by any means necessary!

They have the guns and the bullets, but we provide the targets. Despite how great we know we are; Black Americans are often referred to as lazy people. Ever since we walked off the plantation, and stopped working for free—they've called us lazy. What it means is, ever since we stopped working for free, we're somehow lazy. In reality, the "lazy" affixations white people placed on us—belong to them.

Black people are inventors, musicians, medical professionals, and the list goes on. We are way more than athletes; our people built the United States of America! Blacks have refused to work for less, so the white man calls him lazy. Never should a Black man take a lesser position and have to work their way up; the Black man is already up! So, he deserves a position equivalent to his skill level.

They want to call us needy people; the Black American came into existence in 1865, in the United States of America after the Emancipation Proclamation. That is approximately two hundred years after the start of the United States of America.

Blacks in America got their start 400 years late in the game of life, with nothing but the rags on their backs. If the white man wants to call this needy, then that is fine, especially when the white man has had a 400-year head start in this country.

Blacks came from slavery with nothing and still made it! From wearing rags off the plantation to becoming the most feared and successful race in America, Blacks came out of slavery lacking the cognitive abilities to thrive in the white American system.

White America has a negative view of all Black existence, it describes a ruthless society. One white society buries bodies of infant Black babies up to the neck, then sees which white man can kick the head off the "N-child," white people are willing to sacrifice their young, for position power, land, and property. White men will do this, to gain status, white power, money, and women.

I was born into a Black Mississippi society; I call it "In and Out of Mississippi." In a one-on-one conversation with a white man, I had to describe how it feels to be Black in America. First and foremost, there is no comparison between being Black and being white in Mississippi. If you are Black, you are expected to stay in your "place" (meaning you better not look a white person in the eye, say 'Yassah boss,' and make it your duty to adhere to all elements of Jim Crow) to survive Mississippi.

When the Black man decides to feel equal, better, and proud—it becomes a problem for the white man. The white man, then thinks he is losing his lifetime control over Black people. When Black Lives Matter presents a problem, the white man finds a way to cut off access to mainstream America. It is extremely sad and dysfunctional of a society when the people in power use that power to severely control other people. Some white people in power have grown arrogant, obnoxious, selfish, greedy, liars, and worst of all, bigots. Ask 45.

I had the greatest times living and growing up in Inverness. There were always people to see, friends to hang with, and things to get into. One night while walking the streets of Inverness, it was me, Big Mike, Dirty Red, Bo Bo, and Willie D.

We were walking away from downtown on the right side of the park when Bo Bo said, "Hey man, he was talking to me, Mr. Strong wants to get with you, he likes you and told someone he wanted to get with you."

I said, "Bullshit! Let's find that motherfucker!"

They laughed and thought that comment was funny, I did not. You see, Mr. Strong was the band teacher and I was in the band. He taught me how to play the horn instruments and how to read music fluently. I could see that he was a feminine man but at nine years old, I had no clue he was gay. There was never a discussion in my town about that lifestyle. The Inverness band was awesome, and we could play that funky music. Anyways, we continued to walk the streets of Inverness until we ran up on Mr. Strong, the band director.

Without any hesitation or mental reservation, I ran to his car with my friends holding me back from him.

I said, "Mr. Strong! I am not gay and I do not appreciate you telling someone you want to get with me! I will never come to your class again and I better pass!"

And I quit the band. From that day to this one, I have not been able to gain a rhythm. I lost my ability to play music because I was traumatized by the idea that he wanted to abuse me. If I could, I would have kicked his ass! Keep in mind; I'm in the eighth grade at Inverness Elementary School. I spent the rest of the year in Ms. Brown's class during the band class period. Leaving Inverness with a "C" in Band, I was satisfied. From that day to this one; I never said another word to Mr. Strong. I think he passed away in the year 2000.

This brings me back to the time I had a gay mechanic working for me at Fort Bragg, North Carolina; his name was Private Benjamin; this is before the movie Private Benjamin. Benjamin was a tall skinny Black dude who was a good Army mechanic. I was his motor sergeant; at Alpha Battery $1^{st}/39^{th}$ Field Artillery.

One day the alert came down for the Battery to deploy to the field with all gear and guns in tow. My job as the motor sergeant was to ensure all vehicles were running smoothly and I did, we had excellent vehicles in the battery. Since our mechanics were up on maintenance, we picked up the extra duties to support the cannons when they were on a mission.

One job that I remember, was driving the honey wagon; aka the shit truck. The truck had the responsibility to clean the portable potties from all the campsites while in the field. My co-pilot just happened to be Private Benjamin; I was the truck driver and he was the shit pumper. The duty was not so bad, just had a problem at the time spending so much time in the honey wagon with Private Benjamin.

I eventually gained a lot of respect for him because he was a good mechanic and he did excellent work. He just continued to get on my nerves when he called my name, he would always say Sergeant Smiiiithhh, and it would drive me crazy.

THE MISSISSIPPI DELTA

My hometown of Inverness is nestled thirty-eight miles east of the Mississippi River, ninety miles south of Memphis, and ninety miles northwest of Jackson. The Union Pacific Railroad ran north and south dividing Inverness into whites on the northeast side of the tracks and Blacks on the southwest side of the tracks.

My dad built me a sandbox next to our Jim Walters home when I was around six or seven. I remember sitting and playing with him in the sandbox for the first time. In the sandbox was a dump truck, a road grader, and some kind of loader—all this stuff was off the Tonka brand. I've always thought that playing with my dad in the sandbox was one of the best memories from my childhood.

My dad gave me the first mini bike in the black Inverness community. I rode the hell out of that minibike, so hard that I broke the throttle and had to put a string there to give it the gas. I rode for two or three years before it broke down completely. Then, the natural place to take it was Uncle Roosevelt's Service Station.

There, working at the gas station was Glenn and Charles, the neighborhood mechanic. I expected them to fix it for me even though they were auto mechanics, not mini bike mechanics. They put the bike in the back of the station and told me that they would get around to it.

Before they could fix it, an F-5 tornado hit Inverness and tore the gas station down, along with many homes and buildings. All I could think about was my minibike sitting behind the station. Minutes after the tornado event, even before we found my sister Tenia, I asked Muddear about going to get my minibike from the gas station. She told me to shut up and look for my sister.

I used to walk up to the station to see if Uncle Roosevelt would give me a job so that I could make a little money. I found it very hard to ask for a job there because I felt he would say no. Once, he did give me a job to do. Uncle Roosevelt told me to paint all the fire hydrants on First Street with something happy. Excited to have a job, I went to go buy the paint and the brushes to get it done.

It was a cool summer morning, and I wanted to get started early. I began around nine in the morning and finished at about seven or eight that evening. I went to the station the next day and asked Uncle if he liked the work. He told me that he did and paid me four dollars for the whole day. I was very disappointed but acted happy to have a little money in my pocket.

That day taught me a lesson: always have a clear understanding of salary in any job! Never again did I go to the station looking for work. The payment left me with a sour taste in my mouth about working there. I eventually went to a different gas station, Billie Ed's, for work. Sammy and his dad, Mr. Yank, worked there.

I learned a lot watching Mr. Yank service the white people. When they pulled up, he would spring into action with his rag hanging from his pocket and a cigarette dangling in his mouth. First, he put the gas pump into the car, while the car was filling up; he would check the oil and finish off by cleaning the windshield with a slap of the rag on the window when he finished. With the work done, Mr. Yank would ease smoothly back over to the tire shop until the next one showed up.

Mr. Yank could balance tires on a machine that used his fingers to determine which weight to add to the tire. The machine had a spinning wheel that turned the tire at about fifty miles an hour. A round piece with four chrome-plated knobs used to make adjustments was attached to the tire rim. He slowly tweaked the knobs until he received the least wobble and that was it. Mr. Yank was a cool person who was a great role model. I had the most respect for that man.

During the summer, the boys organized real baseball teams with uniforms. Snake, aka Willie Earl Langston, played first, I played second and Sammy or Kirk Price played shortstop, Michael Thomas was the catcher and Big Mike played third base. Michael Thomas was known for scooping up a glove full of dirt with the ball, he had no problem getting in the dirt. Snake, could play some baseball, stretching nearly half the distance to catch a ball thrown to first base. Dwaine was our pitcher.

We practiced every day after school and traveled to other towns to play. On a baseball trip to Drew, Mississippi, I knocked in a couple of runners batted in (RBI) hitting my first home run. Mr. Jessie Stanger played a significant part in our baseball season; he let us travel to games in an old raggedy Chevy station wagon. He also let us use it to drive around during the summer. Thank you, Mr. Jessie. There were others we knew that influenced our lives:

- Mr. Jimmy Liggins slaughtered hogs and chickens.
- Mr. Booker Denton drove the field truck.
- LV and Billy were the baseball coaches. They were my inspiration for baseball and team sports. Without them, I do not think there would have been an Inverness baseball team.
- Mr. Yank was smooth Sammy's daddy and the gas station attendant
- Uncle Roosevelt was the first Black man to own a gas station in Inverness.
- Sam Bo was a cool man that always crept around town with his wrist lapped over the steering wheel.
- Hulk was the man nobody played with. I guess that's why they called him the Hulk. He was also the neighborhood mechanic.
- Uncle UW was a good, one-legged man who always let me drive his 1966 Chevy. I often went to him for advice.
- Frank Bailey was a quiet, grumpy type, but was always nice to me.
- Mr. Jab was the sport fisherman around town.
- Eddie C. was my first cousin's dad and a mentor to me.
- Mr. Slim was the Inverness strong man. I watched this man drive over fifty poles in the ground with a sledgehammer and a two-by-four. He stood nearly seven feet tall and always wore overalls with no shirt.
- Mr. Frog who I remember as a very nice person.

- Mr. Dessie was another nice guy who showed me how to be a man.
- Dossy Lee was the town policeman who always tried to help. Back then, a policeman was a friend first and a cop second.
- And last but not least, was Stick, his leg was permanently in a bending position and he walked with a crutch.

There were more influences, but this list is who I remember.

Daily wages were less than six dollars for an entire day. The day would start early in the morning when Muddear woke us up. In those days and even today, we still call our mother Muddear and our grandmother mamma. I have yet to figure out how this name came to be, but that is another story.

I always wanted to make my own money because it was too hard for my Muddear to support the five of us on her income and I wanted to be independent enough to support myself. Muddear would wake me around five in the morning. I had time to get myself together and be out the door at five forty-five, the field truck would pass by my house around that time.

Tenia and Wes, short for Wesley, would already be up and ready for the truck; they had to push me along. When the truck came to a short stop in front of the house, it was already loaded with about ten bodies so we had to push our way on board while the truck was starting to pull off again. On the way to the next stop, I had to find a cozy corner to get more sleep on the way to the cotton field.

It was a cool ride in the Mississippi morning on the way to the cotton field. The cool ride would soon be overcome by the blistering sun coming up over the horizon. Every day it would get so hot that when you looked over the acres and acres of cotton, you could see the heat waves looking like water on dry land. When the truck left Inverness, we headed to the cotton fields in the country (a few miles outside of Inverness).

When the truck hit the field, everyone rushed to get off the truck and grab a hoe, these tools were the best pickings for the people on the truck; many of the old school choppers had a special hoe. If you grabbed the wrong one, they would take it from you. Old school gets the good hoes if you are a good old school cotton chopper. The worker with little experience ended up with a dull and hard-to-use hoe.

A couple of the cotton choppers were our water boys; they had a galvanized bucket and a metal cup. Everyone drank from the same cup back then, no questions asked but the water was good and cold. It was a refreshing sight to see the water boys halfway down that row of cotton. The rows were nearly a mile long and when you reached the end you turned around and went down another row back towards the truck. A "file boy" was also assigned to go from one side to the other sharpening everybody's hoe.

The Delta is an agricultural land base that covers the basin where the Mississippi River once ran and deposited the fertile soil. From the '50s through the '70s, every Black in the Mississippi Delta had something to do with cotton. Blacks tilled the soil, planted the seeds, and plowed the fields. We picked the cotton then ginned it, baled it, and shipped it. Blacks were the cheap labor that made the white plantation owners millionaires. To this day, the white plantation owners strive to keep poor Blacks as their source of labor. It was that way then and it is that way now.

Tight was one of the many nicknames for the field master, Booker Denton. He was responsible for getting the cotton choppers to the field, paying them wages, and making sure they didn't cut down any cotton stalks. When he'd tell everyone to line up, we would scramble to a row that looked clean just to find that there was lots of grass to cut over the bend.

Once we lined up, he would say, "Move out and stay on the line."

The method proved to be successful for him. About forty Black people would be bent over a hoe trying to get that row out. Tight was always the one we kept our eye on. We could see him anywhere in the field because he kept a hoe on his shoulder.

Most of the time Tight had a deal with the white man. He would take his cut from each of the choppers on his truck. If we were making $30 a day for chopping cotton, he would take anywhere from $5 to $15. It boiled down to Tight making a lot of money off the backs of the cotton choppers. The white man was paying him as well, so he was getting money from both sides. I commend him for being an entrepreneur, but he could have helped the black people more.

Many conversations were going on in the cotton field. There were mothers, fathers, sisters, brothers, uncles, aunts, siblings, cousins, friends, and enemies—all in a line strung out across the cotton field. For a time, I was there too, talking and listening. This is how the gossip moved around town: what was going on with the white man, who died, who got shot, who is cheating on who, and who the preacher is trying to screw. As a young man, it was a good opportunity to meet girls. My friends were all trying to find the girls that the mothers were watching, and sometimes we got lucky.

One summer night, Sammy, Willie D., Big Mike, and I were walking down the streets as we usually did. Sammy and Willie D. started talking about stealing something, and I told them that it was not a good idea. We came down the muddy road in between the cotton gin—a road we walked almost every night just because they told us not to. When we made it to Duncan Gin Road, we turned right towards my house. Big Mike dropped off when we made it to his house across from the intersection. The rest of us took a right turn towards Uncle Roosevelt's gas station.

After their arrest and release, Sammy told me the story. He and Willie D. went into the station through a bathroom window. While at the cash register, Willie D dropped some change on the floor. He was picking it up off the floor when he heard someone at the Coke machine at the front of the office. It was Little Frog, which was a nickname for Patrick Thomas. About the time when Frog was turning to leave, Willie D. raised his head. He and Frog looked in the eyes. Frog took off in a sprint, running to go tell on them. Next thing you know, Sammy and Willie D. were in jail for robbery. Sammy could only laugh at the situation because they both knew that it was a stupid idea.

We were always into something around that little town of Inverness. Walking down the railroad tracks was a favorite summer day activity. We followed the big boys—Wes, Tommy Steve, Booker T, and Dee—down the tracks until they threw rocks to turn us away. After that, we still followed them but at a greater distance. This is how we found Acapulco, the neighborhood swimming hole.

Acapulco was a beautiful stream about six feet deep, fifteen feet wide, and twenty-five feet long. Trees surrounded it and hung over the water. The temperature could be over a hundred degrees on the way there, but the water was always nice and cool. I learned how to swim at that place, taught by the one and only Larry Brown. During the summer, we went to Acapulco every day to cool down from the hot and humid Mississippi weather.

Segregation Now, Segregation Forever: Mississippi Style

Segregation in Mississippi is real and exists from every corner of the state, so do not think the struggle is over, it is as real as it gets in Mississippi. We eat in our restaurants and live our lives without venturing to the white side of town unless we are working for the white man.

Segregation started after the abolishment of slavery. Three constitutional amendments were passed to grant freed Blacks legal status: the 13th Amendment abolished slavery, the 14th provided citizenship, and the 15th guaranteed the right to vote. Despite these amendments, the Supreme Court made decisions between 1873 and 1883 that killed the work of Congress. Blacks were still seen as property and couldn't access the services available to other Americans.

Only about 3,500 Black families laid claim to the US General Land Office's land grants. Specifically, the Exodusters who famously settled Kansas. During the Western migration, America's population moved towards California. The government gave white immigrants plots of land called homesteads, with access to farm the land. Black, Asian, Mexican, and Native American domestic workers often found themselves on the receiving end of discriminatory practices when it came to getting more land grants. Local law enforced the separation of Blacks and Whites in all areas of life. In 1896 the Supreme Court held up its ruling in *Plessy v. Ferguson*, for separate but equal facilities. There is a line of connection for Blacks in these rulings present from 1986 through the modern Civil Rights Movement—it is up to us to see them.

The Civil Rights Acts of 1964 & 1965 brought a small measure of equality to Black Americans. However, it would take some time for the act to bring about real change. It was in 2017 when I saw the thread that binds us as a country, tempted to break. Not much separates or changes the way Black and white America operates from the era before 1964 except there are more Blacks with money.

Initially, the Civil Rights movement was meant to change the way white people treated, acted, played, respected, served, and lived by Black people. Before our Black leaders could catch up and understand what was happening, the Civil Rights Movement shifted from getting equal or better rights for Blacks to affording more rights for white women. The movement was hijacked from Black people before serving the cause.

Blacks started the movement in the 1960s and white women saw the potential for change with them as the new "minorities," during the 1970s and 1980s. It gave time to the White Knights of the Ku Klux Klan to bolster visibility, recruitment and to set new plates of power at their dinner tables. The more things change, the more things stay the same.

If the opportunity ever presented itself for slave trading, I am convinced our children would be on the slave auction blocks across the USA. There is a reason that in Fayetteville, North Carolina, on Hay Street, there is a restored slave auction block in the center of the street. This slave auction stand was burned, crashed, and paint splashed; each time the city of Fayetteville restored it to mint condition.

The unspoken notion of Blacks in slavery is evident all the time in America, it feels like a racehorse in the start gate, it feels like a diver with his toes on the tallest board and it feels like a race car on the pace lap waiting for the green flag. People, there is only one way to circumvent the momentum of abolishing the Civil Rights Movement and its acts, that is to unite and follow a common goal! Stop the separation in our "Black races" and unite with a leader and with a cause. Join something, set an agenda, and do not be like the two Blacks in the White House; Clarence Thomas and surgeon Ben Carson.

The number one priority is to keep the Black dollar circulating in the Black Business Community (i.e., Spend your Black dollars at Black businesses at all costs). The best thing we can do when it comes to the economy is to stop the undirected spending of our money. Every first Tuesday is "Black Out Tuesday;" do not spend any money outside of the Black community, in other words, spend only with Black businesses.

MAKE BLACK PEOPLE INVISIBLE AGAIN

Under the Civil Rights Act of 1964, segregation on the grounds of race, religion, or national origin was banned at all public place accommodation, including courthouses, parks, restaurants, theaters, sports arenas, and hotels. No longer could Blacks and other minorities be denied service based on the color of their skin, according to the 1964 Act, that is. With the backing of the government, on paper, Blacks had every right of a citizen in the United States of America.

As we so deeply wanted to believe; there was no way that a southern white man would see himself as equal with a Black man. They have been taught for centuries and from birth, that Black people are renters, not owners of anything and that Black people can never meet or match a white person. The average wealth of a Black household is 83 % lower than that of the average white household.

In other words, the white man has always been the devil during the hours of darkness and your employer during regular business hours. The white man created the Jim Crow laws and knight riders, AKA, the Ku Klux Klan (KKK). Blacks did not venture across the tracks after dark, it was and, in some places, still is segregation in true form.

As a child growing up in Mississippi, I had no idea what my mother and forefathers had to endure every day dealing with white people. As they did to George Floyd, the white man has his knee on the neck of every Black Man living in Inverness.

I grew up listening to the blues but I also remember listening to the don'ts. Do not go over there by the bayou during the daytime talking about going fishing, especially after dark; the bayou was reserved for the whites. The Bayou, which is what we called it, was a slow-moving stream separating most of the so-called "high-class white folks" from the Black side of town.

Every year, month, day, hour and through every second of all recorded time and the existence of the Black man, white men have been trying to suppress them. As far back as the thirteen colonies, white men have denied Blacks equal or better recognition of everything. During the Revolutionary War, the Civil War, and the Civil Rights Movement, Black men gave way to others.

First, Blacks gave way to the immigrant colonists, Amerikkka opened its borders and said "give me your white poor, and hungry" from all over the world and they came. Each year, Amerikkka made fifty to one hundred thousand white immigrants citizens of Amerikka while at the same time denying any progress for Blacks already here in Amerikkka. After giving the country away to immigrants, it was the southern whites and finally, to white women.

How can Amerikkka take a Black, revolutionary movement, The Civil Rights Movement, to gain better representation in America and turn it into a "thing" for the white woman's fight to have equal rights? The worst part about it is that society turned from getting better rights for Blacks to getting better rights for white women. No matter what the Black man starts, initiates building on, invents, or creates it was taken by white people and made theirs.

I have tried to not end up with this belief about Amerikkka, but each time and each incident, the results are always the same; Black people are increasingly disenfranchised, apathetic, and afraid to fight for their past, present and future. The farther we get from Minister Malcolm X and the year 1964, the weaker the culture gets. There are no significant leaders in the path of our future who are taking the lead in the new civil rights movement.

Yes, the new civil rights movement is revisiting the road to equality and better. To complete the mission of the 1964 efforts, a new aggressive movement is starting to catch steam. The efforts put forth by the white women's right to affirmative action in the 1970s and 80s as a newly defined minority is a major example. This time, while the Black Lives Matter Movement catches steam, I can see other civil rights movements trying to tag along and take a stake in the revolution alongside the Black Movement.

Every time Black people try to do something here they come, sometimes I feel like they (other movements) hinder the Black

Agenda rather than help it along. However, it was the George Floyd killing that ignited a new wave of protests across the nation seeking change, including the introduction of the George Floyd Act in Congress.

It is time for each of us to review the Civil Rights Act of 1964 line by line. Each line of the Act is not about the Black man however, many of them are. This situation and results of this act left us again, hoodwinked and bamboozled about what is equal or better for the Black man in white America. I am sick and tired of losing this fight against bettering the Black race. The more we do to get close to the prize, we get derailed by someone else's agenda.

Marcus Garvey, Emmitt Till, Martin L. King Jr., Malcolm X, and Medgar Evers, the last Black men assassinated were on to something. The FBI (Federal Bureau of Investigation) destroyed the Black Panther Party which created breakfast programs to feed poor children and inspired Congress into action with their creation of the WIC (Women, Infants, and Children) program in 1972, then made permanent in 1975. Overall, the policies and stringent rules informed me that giving us welfare, housing assistance, assisted living, WIC, free medical for women, and transportation vouchers— was all an effort to shut us up. Only to the women who "swear" to keep Black men out of the household kept their income and benefits. The Black women are threatened to be cut off if a Black man is caught in their residence the government pays for.

So, let us recap if the Black woman allows a Black man into their homes that the government pays for, they will be evicted, no questions asked (turning the Black woman against the Black man). They help to elect incompetent leaders to prolong the problem (voter suppression). Rarely do we elect the right person, most of the time? Oh yes, we are entitled, we are entitled to an open door to the top of any circle we decide to travel in. When the gates were opened, the Black man was left standing still, not by choice. We were still oppressed and enslaved by the white man by his policies.

Blacks were not allowed to move freely for nearly 400 years. While the white man claimed the land, Blacks were simply denied access to owning land. Every state outside of the thirteen colonies was game for white men to claim, for pennies on the dollar. An acre of land cost one penny when bought from the government. The government sold acres by the thousands and the Black man was not invited to the sale.

Before Abraham Lincoln won the Civil War, his General William Tecumseh Sherman, feared by racists, granted each freed family forty acres and a mule in South Carolina with military provision Special Field Order #15. Days after the ruling to honor former slaves with a land grant, President Lincoln was assassinated. The assumed President Andrew Johnson, an avowed racist, rescinded the forty-acre order, therefore, removing the only edge up Blacks have ever had in Amerikkka.

To this day in 2020, nothing on that level has ever been done to help Blacks gain a foothold in Amerikkka. More has been done to suppress everything about the Black man. No other serious reparations have been offered or proposed since 1865. Now it is 2020, American Blacks have the highest high school to prison conviction rate in the world. Most Blacks have no wealth, no land, and many are ignorant of their heritage.

What is expected by society is for Black people to be happy that we are free, hell to the naw; we will never be happy until reparations are paid! The white man received a 400-year head start with the government's assistance. The government acts as if it is the innocent party in the room, but in reality, the government is the cause of the Black man's demise. It is like a well-planned and executed scheme. A little nod here, a nudge there and a wink are all it took to kill the Black man's American dream—even with their finances affected by the nuances of racism via policy.

THE BLUES IS ALRIGHT

The B.B. King Museum

I am sure you have heard of the Blues Crossroad. Many people claim to have the "crossroads" in their town, but I can prove it is definitely in Indianola, Mississippi. An exhibit in the B.B. King Museum and Delta Interpretive Center talks about the crossroads being in Indianola.

When you walk into the museum, don't forget to sign the visitor's book. The first stop is a ten-minute movie about B.B. King and his ties to the Mississippi Delta. Next, you will see a historic cotton sack hanging on the wall along with thousands of other artifacts from his time in Mississippi. At the end of a walk-through history, you will see his eleven Grammy Awards. Outside, you can see his bus and a memorial gravesite for him. There is also a gift shop with lots of good souvenirs to take back home.

There is a brick building attached to the museum that was once a cotton gin dating back to 1905. Many Blacks worked there for very little pay. When the cotton industry slowed down, the gin closed. It is said to be the oldest cotton gin still standing in the state of Mississippi.

Processing Cotton in the Mississippi Delta

The Delta is the agricultural hub of Mississippi, and Indianola is practically the center of those plantations. In this region, Black people are the underdogs and the readily available workforce. Until recently, Black workers were the only ones available to keep the cotton fields pruned and groomed. Now, Mexicans are taking over the plantation work in the Delta. Children are working the fields as early as six years old. They sometimes spend an entire life working in the fields for the white man.

The Inverness cotton gin is a business where we as Blacks work for the white man. A Black man on a tractor picks cotton from the fields. Blacks with their sacks could pick cotton right alongside the tractor. Before the tractor, Black workers were the only way to get the cotton out of the field.

Cotton from the field must go through a refining process. After picking, the cotton is put into a trailer and transported to the Black neighborhood in Inverness for processing at the Duncan's Gin.

Once it reaches the gin, the cotton is vacuumed up through a pipe that separates the cotton from the seeds and trash. The usable cotton is baled into five-hundred-pound bales. The seeds are put into fifty-pound bags.

The trash is sent to an incinerator located in a Black neighborhood, not even a hundred yards from the house where I grew up. The incinerator spews Black smoke from a gigantic smokestack in all directions. I am not surprised that many people from Inverness have died from lung-related diseases.

I have seen Black men come into Ludie's Café in Inverness covered from head to toe in dust. There is no doubt that he was on a tractor plowing, planting, or cultivating a cotton field. These men look beaten as if they have nothing else to live for. I have noticed that there is a difference between a white Mississippian and a Black Mississippian; that is, the Blacks are psychologically damaged for life. There is no therapy or counseling available to repair the damage that the white people have caused Black men and their families.

Growing Up in Inverness: Woodshop, Band, and Boy Scouts

Inverness had a lot to offer growing up in the 1970s. The band, the woodshop, and the Boy Scouts kept me very busy as I grew into a teenager in the Mississippi Delta.

The basketball coach, Mr. Howard, ran the woodshop and taught us how to build a little bit of everything. In the woodshop, we built storage rooms, runways for the Miss 349 Beauty Pageant, and walls from the floor up. Mr. Howard also taught us the basics of electricity and plumbing, so we had working knowledge about construction.

When I was in the band, I started out learning how to play the cornet in the band and ended on a baritone horn. I also played the trumpet and the French horn. I could read music and play those instruments very well!

Larry Brown and I were the baselines for the horn department. When we played in a parade in Memphis, we had to march a five-mile route. As we marched, the drumline somehow went off-beat during a song. Larry and I kept that baritone horn on beat, on note, and in harmony. We put the band back on point with that horn sound. That was one proud moment.

I can truly say that I loved being a Boy Scout. I was a Scout Master in San Antonio from 2009 until 2016. During that time, I taught nearly thirty boys how to be outdoorsmen, five of who became Eagle Scouts. We learned how to march, tie knots, shoot guns, shoot bows, camp, cook on a campfire, and other things that prepared them for life in the great outdoors.

In the Boy Scouts, we camped out in the forest behind the school. One day, we were trying to cook an egg on a gallon jug that we repurposed as a stove. Then, the jug tipped over and spilled grease onto my hand. This incident left a huge, painful blister on my hand, but I continued with the trip.

Each time we went camping, we had to set up WWII Army tents. We had to snap the pieces together, balance the three poles in the center, and stake it down. Sammy and I were always tent mates. One time, I told Sammy to blow out his candle before he fell asleep; he fussed back and said that he would. About an hour later, the candle had burned out and the tent was on fire! He was still asleep, so I grabbed the foot of his sleeping bag and pulled him out fast. All he could do was giggle as he so often did.

During a summer in the late seventies, I remember going to Camp Talahaw in Grenada and attending many jamborees. This is where earning merit badges was a top priority. By the end of the week at Camp Talahaw, I had earned almost thirty badges. I achieved the rank of Life Scout but gave up on getting the Eagle Scout requirements done.

The Boy Scouts was my salvation; I thrived doing it. One Saturday at the mall in Greenville, we set up a lookout tower by lacing and lashing it all together. People in the mall watched us in awe. It was a magnificent day for me and my troop as we displayed what we could do with ropes and trees.

Making My Own Money

Summer in Inverness was hot and isolated. Sammy, Big Mike, and I would usually get together early in the morning. Sometimes, we'd go over to the white side of town to mow yards, cut hedges, and clean up yards. I used to work for a retired schoolteacher, Ms. Hunter, who was cheap as hell. This woman paid me ten dollars to cut her half-acre yard with my push mower. I quit after that.

After about a week, Ms. Hunter came to my house and parked at the end of the driveway. Muddear sent Tenia out to see what she wanted. She wanted me to return to work, saying that she would pay me more money. I took the offer, and she started paying me well. As a bonus, she gave me a classic Yazoo mower, the one with the balloon tires on the back. That lawnmower made me a lot of money over the years.

It was important for me to buy my clothes every year for high school. Muddear had a lot on her plate, so I made sure to take care of myself, hustling every way I knew how. At the age of fifteen, I took that money and decided to flip it.

I had Tommy Steve take me to Greenville to score a brick of weed for a hundred dollars. We made it back to Inverness, separated the brick into nickel bags, and put the bags into a shoebox. I stood on the corner near Mr. Kemp's grocery, selling weed right in front of Mr. Otis, the town sheriff. He never confronted me, so I made around four hundred a week from that process.

Swimming in the Local Waters

I had my own friends and my older brothers, Click and Wes had theirs. They did not want my friends and me around much, so they threw rocks at us when we followed them down the railroad tracks. Rocks were especially thrown when it was that time of day when we went to Acapulco, the local swimming hole. Most of the time when we made it to the hole, the older boys would move on to their next mission.

When we walked the railroad tracks, we picked blackberries, hunted rabbits, and hung out at the train trestle. A train trestle is a bridge that goes over a small body of running water. As boys, we used the trestle as a diving platform for the muddy water below.

One day while sitting on the trestle drying out after a swim, I saw a leech sucking the blood out of Larry's foot. He tried to pull it off but couldn't, so he took a match and lit the leech on fire. It came off and left a trickle of Larry's blood running down his feet. That was the last time I got in the water.

About a month later, Huh Huh Talha, Dennis, and Sammy went to the trestle for a swim. The water was high and running fast. They jumped in, but Huh Huh did not make it out. He drowned that day. It took law enforcement several days to find his bloated body. Huh Huh was the only one I can remember drowning as a result of all the swimming we did over the summers in Inverness.

We also swam in Macon Lake where the water was clear and calm. There was a pier running out about twenty feet. Near the shore, there was a rope that we used to swing out over the water and drop onto our inner tubes. We would get on the tubes and float on the lake all day long. It was a lot of fun for a summer evening among friends.

One day, we decided to swim across the whole lake. It was sixty to eighty feet wide, but that meant nothing to us. We were all good swimmers except for Sammy; he loved the water but could not swim a lick. Everyone went across the lake in pairs. The first pair was Larry and Clark, who made it across. The next pair was Mike and Eugene.

When they got halfway across, Eugene gave up. He hurled himself out of the water and onto Mike's back, and they started to sink. A few seconds later, Big Mike shot from under the water and Eugene came up after him. He reached for Mike, but Mike kept his distance and started coaching him across the lake. He almost gave up and drowned, but he made it! The next pair was me and Bo Bo, but we did not go through with it after watching Eugene struggle.

Macon Lake was for Black people on Sundays and white people on Saturdays. We never mixed at the lake. If we went and the white kids were there, we kept it moving. Sammy, with his yellow ass, decided to go on down to the lake and hang out with the white folks. He was the only one of us with enough balls to go in the water with them.

By now, tubing has become commercialized. I don't blame them; the business makes a lot of money. But, back in the 1960s, we drove to Macon Lake with our inner tubes strapped to the top of Mr. Jessie's old station wagon. That wagon didn't have a muffler, so you could hear us coming down the road.

NATIVE BLACK AMERICANS MATTER

Pre-Columbian African Settlements in the Americas

Thousands of years before Columbus came to the New World, Black people had come from across the Atlantic Ocean. However, in our public schools, they still teach us nonsense about Columbus discovering America! It is up to us to know and find the truth. Blacks were here already.

The discovery of Olmec statues proves the existence of pre-Columbian African settlements in the Americas. Found in Central and South America, these huge stone statues depict human faces with African facial features—often helmeted men with full lips, broad noses, and large eyes. They can be up to eleven feet tall and weigh forty tons.

Olmec Head Statue

Native Black Americans Today

The Native Black Americans are the descendants of slaves who were born in the United States. Today, Blacks come from Puerto Rico, Mexico, Africa, and China—from every continent on the planet. Blacks, other than native Black Americans, have entitlements due because of our heritage here that was hidden and destroyed. We are born as citizens while others are naturalized.

Native Blacks do not need passports or special qualifications to work, but the others do. Native Blacks living in the Mississippi Delta were exploited. White people had us working in the fields—plowing, planting, and nurturing crops. They had us in the house—cleaning up after them and taking care of their children. Children worked in the yard as yard boys—cleaning gutters, clipping hedges, and mowing lawns.

Where I grew up, Native Blacks attended Woodburn Elementary School out on the Mound, a small community outside of Inverness. Woodburn was a one-room shack for all ages of students. There was no public funding, so the teachers had to supply the materials for their students. But, back then, students only needed a number two pencil and a piece of paper. My grandmother, Genella Faint, worked as a teacher at the school.

The Native Blacks received poor medical care in the Mississippi Delta. Dr. Yoo was a Chinese doctor working in the Indianola hospital servicing older people. Rumor was, you should never go to that hospital because they would kill you with the poor medical care. My mother died there on April 23, 2017. In my opinion, she died because of negligence from the staff. Usually, the doctors, who were white or Asian, made money off the backs of poor and elderly Black people.

Native Black people were bred to tend the dirt on plantations. They received less than the minimum wage and did not complain about it. Native Black people in the Mississippi Delta have severe mental damage. Most suffer from PTSD and don't know it.

The Cycle of Poverty in Plantation Life

White-owned plantations rule the land in the Mississippi Delta. They own almost all the wealth, which they achieve by employing a Black workforce to farm their land. White plantation owners have kept land ownership out of Black hands for the last five hundred years.

Row houses were the only available housing for our people on the plantation. Black men who worked the fields would raise their families in one of those houses, but they'd have to pay rent. They'd also buy groceries and borrow money "on the books" at the plantation store. On the plantation, the store is most likely run by the white man's family.

Black people make very little money for the work they do on the plantation, so they never have enough money to enjoy a paycheck or save a dime. They get their paychecks from the plantation's store or from the white man in the field. If a Black man goes to the store for his paycheck, the clerk may say that he owes the store money "on the books," even if he doesn't. This can easily cut down your net pay for the week, but the Black man cannot question the math of the storekeeper. He has to believe, or act as if he believes, that the math is accurate. He knows that it's a rip-off but doesn't know how to go about proving it, so he leaves it alone.

A Black man may use up his future paychecks in advance if his family still needs to eat. This is how they enter into a cycle of poverty and indebtedness to the white man. Now, the Black family has no other choice but to use the plantation's store to feed him and his family.

So, he'll say, "Put it on the books."

This practice is still in use today. Even though it gives poor people an opportunity to have something to eat, it does more harm than good. The way I see it, the storekeeper wants to put charges "on the books" so that, on payday, he can deduct what he wants from his workers' checks. This is how they enter a cycle of poverty and indebtedness to the white man. It is a vicious cycle that keeps poor people poor as the wealthy profit from their lives.

If a tractor driver's son decides to live on the plantation with his family but work elsewhere, the white man will make him move off the plantation. Why? Because the white plantation bosses want the next generation of Black kids to grow up on the plantation and take their father's place. If the father gets hurt and cannot work, the family will need to move. The Black man has to move his family off the plantation so the white man can move in with his next unsuspecting Black family.

No Black makes enough money to gain stability in the Mississippi Delta. The wages are low and regulated to keep Blacks poor. I remember the time I worked an eight-hour day and received

$5 for the entire shift. Other times we received $7 a day for working on the cotton chopping wagon.

That was when I realized that leaving Mississippi was not an option, it was necessary. Daily wage dictates the living standards. Most family housing in the Delta was dilapidated and did not comply with regulations and building codes.

White Men's Relationship with Black Women

White men often speak of Black women's beauty—especially light-skinned women—in a very flattering and erotic way. A Black woman has an advantage without even trying. There is a natural beauty within the Black woman, so all men want to know them. It is nobody's fault that our sisters are so beautiful.

Why is it that all mixed-race babies are classified as Black? It is a conditioned society that states if two percent of a child is Black, then the baby is Black. If a child has a white father and a Black mother, the child is Black. If a child has a white mother and a Black father, the child is still Black. Any child born with mixed parents automatically assumes the Black race.

In this day and age, Black women and men want to have kids with the white race just to create a child with blue eyes and fine hair. This is not politically correct. There is more than just heartbreak at stake here, this is not the way to maintain traditions and cultures. In America, and abroad, we see pictures in the media with many white males who know the value of a Black woman over a white woman.

White men often give employment preference to Black women over Black men. If a Black woman works hard, is great at what she does, getting moved up the ladder in corporate America is no hill she cannot climb. It is a damn shame that in this century, Black men are what white men fear the most.

The sad part is when the Black woman starts to believe the lies coming from the white man's mouth. Not all Black women fall for the Okie-Doke, but many of them do. If only they knew that this is a setup to get them working against the Black man in the white man's favor.

Many of us see it every day at work, in shopping centers around town, and in our social environments. With the Black man further cut out of the American Dream, it is implied that the Black woman is the head of the household and the breadwinner. This is just another way the white man tries to cut the Black man's throat and put a nail in the Black man's coffin. It is an attempt to make him less significant in the world and in the family.

As a boy growing up in the Mississippi Delta, I felt trapped. I thought that I would have to follow the same path as many Black men who went down this road before me. Somehow, I knew that I had to break out of the plantation's cruel cycle of human trafficking. Black women also need to recognize the cycle that the white man has put them in. Black women have the right to love and marry whomever they like, but there is a good Black man somewhere who will marry and love her.

COTTON, MORE IMPORTANT THAN PEOPLE

The town of Inverness divides centrally by a railroad track running down the middle of town. We lived across the street from Duncan's Cotton Gin, the largest cotton gin in the Delta at the time. There were times when the gin ran twenty-four hours a day nonstop. It had a loud pitched whining noise that one never forgets. It sounded like high-speed turbines running at 10,000 +RPM (revolutions per minute).

The cotton season runs from October through December. The Duncan Cotton Gin had to process thousands of trailers full of cotton from local plantations. Hundreds of cotton trailers got parked everywhere there was an open space on the Black side of town. They lined every street and every alley; no illegal parking here cried the police.

Cotton plantations came in from miles around with picked cotton for processing at Duncan Gin of Inverness. Duncan Gin had the biggest pieces of machinery, they processed the most cotton in the Delta, and they hired mostly Black men in Inverness. The men worked on the mechanized switchboards. Functionally, they controlled everything from hooking up a tractor to pulling cotton trailers in for vacuuming.

As a boy, we would sneak around the trailers at night, sometimes jumping from trailer to trailer. Drivers often parked them close together, and we had lots of fun in the cotton trailers. Black women were busy capitalizing on the twenty-four-hour operation. The women brought food in cars, trucks, and vans selling plates. They parked out front of the gin area and made a good salary selling plates all day and night.

This machinery was in an area the size of a modern-day football field. Built of roofing tin on all sides and on top, it was a silver giant in the little town. Surrounding plantations brought the cotton in forty-foot trailers on four wheels rising about fifteen feet high. When a trailer pulled up to the suction tube at the gin, Mr. Stick, a peg-legged Black man went to work. On one crutch, he jumped in the trailer, grabbed the large ring of the suction tube, and began swinging it back and forth across, sucking up the cotton. Going into the tube and thrashers, the separation of the seeds, shells, and dirt left the cotton lily-white. The cotton went one way in the gin and the dirt and seeds went another; the cotton was then compacted into a 500-pound bale.

I could hear this big ass thumper every fifteen seconds sounding like "WHAM WHAM WHAM!" While this was going on, the Black man had to thread the five bands around the bale dodging the WHAM each time he slid the band through the slots. There were rumors that one could easily lose an arm fooling with those bands; only the experienced Black men would do that job.

My crew was busy hopping trailers; that is climbing into the cotton trailers and jumping to the next one. I was too young to work at the cotton gin at the time but as a boy, the cotton gin seemed like the job every kid wanted. Growing up in Inverness, I could see why that was the only thing going on that paid money a Black man could save. I am so glad I never got locked into that program designed to keep the Black man down.

I worked at Ludlow for two weeks, just long enough to get a check and then I quit. The Ludlow was a cotton gin on a smaller scale. I figured I could handle the small cotton gin better than Duncan's. My job was the trucker; the trucker caught the bale of cotton after compression, banding, and the burn. A hammer knocked the bale out of the compressor onto a little cart with me on the handle keeping it from running away. Once I became strong enough to withstand the vibration from catching bales, the next step was more challenging. I had to push it up a ramp about 250ft away at a slight incline. The hardest part was yet to come; the bale had to be stood up on the back of a flatbed truck stacked side by side and two by two. The truck would hold about ten bales.

I would never wish a job like that on anyone white or Black, the work was too hard. A friend who had a nickname of "Fat-Punk" lost three fingers not being fast enough with the bale bands. You see, once you stick and start the band around the bale, you have to get out of the way. The compressing hammer will soon let go; adding about two thousand pounds of compression to the bale's five bands. Fat-Punk was just too slow getting his hand out of the way.

Blacks supplied the labor for everything in America; it would not be an understatement to say Blacks and Indians built this country. It took the Mississippi legislature less than a year to pass a series of laws designed to subjugate freed Black Americans. The Black Codes used an expansive definition of vagrancy and severely restricted the lives of Freedmen after 1865. Simple movements, like walking at night and even evening prayer meetings could result in arrest. The Black Codes made it easy to conflict with the law, the Black man had to shut up and fly very low under the radar of whites. Law enforcement used the Black Codes to systematically arrest Blacks for nothing at all. Before long, the prison population of freed Blacks in Mississippi surged.

There was no prison system large enough to accommodate the arrest rate in Mississippi. So, the state started to release the prisoners to plantation owners for labor. The Union Army burned the state penitentiary in Jackson in 1863; it was only for housing white prisoners. The so-called master had always disciplined Blacks on the plantation.

Once the law started to jail Black men at a higher rate after Reconstruction, the white man figured out that money was being lost. The state needed a way to contain accused Black prisoners. Therefore, it started leasing the Blacks out to plantation owners, railroad builders, and lumber mills. In exchange, the white man paid a small fee to the state and covered the convicts' cost of living.

There were two reasons for Parchman's Penitentiary, one was money-making on the rental of the freed slaves and the other was to maintain racial control over the Black man. Parchman used the chain gang in support of the state labor requirements. For a Black man, the chain gang was the destiny if the plantations did not get you first. In late 1868, many southern prisons began leasing convicts to plantations and industries. As the majority of inmates were Black, this new form of compulsory labor helped to bridge the gap between the Black Codes and Jim Crow. Together, they formed a new reign of social control.

Prisoners Working on the Plantation

If a Black man had a child every year, the white man was very happy with the dad. Back then, Black men found themselves praised for having children, all for the white man! Having more babies born Black made more able body future workers for the fields and more money. Black Boys as young as eight learned how to betray their fathers. The boy's betrayal of their fathers started with them becoming loyal to the white plantation owners. They had it down to a science; the white man befriended the Black kids by giving them something every time he came around. This way, the Black kids would be happy to see the white man. The only problem with that is the white man is coming around to see the Black man's wife and his daughters.

It only takes a candy bar or a cheap toy, they used the same tactic to gain trust on other continents, like when the Portuguese started the Middle Passage slave trade in Africa. Black women could have been at the big house cooking and holding together two families; while the man was out in the fields slaving for the white man. This is when he would circle back to the Black man's house and have sex with his plantation hand's wife. First, the white man checked on the fields making sure that daddy was in a field far away on the other side of the plantation.

This reminds me of another story in the Bible; when David remained in the village and his troops were away in battle, he saw

Bathsheba washing herself. He had sex with her, she became pregnant, and David started his lie to God. David then summoned Bathsheba's husband from battle to entice him to go home and have sex with his wife. The husband slept outside the gate and did not have sex with his wife stating that he felt loyalty to his fellow soldiers, meaning David's army was still in battle where he felt he should be with them.

David now had to devise a white man's plan; he gave Bathsheba's husband a note and sent him back to war. When he arrived back at the war front and gave the officer the note from David, the officer asked, did you read this note? The man replied no; the note stated to put this man in the heat of battle so that he may be killed (2 Samuel 11:15 *NKJV*).

Eventually, Bathsheba had the child and God took him, the end of the story; I could tell the story in detail but this is not a bible lesson. The Black man's wife would not tell it, rather she might say that the boss came by today. She knows the Black man would not ask her why he came by the house because he could not handle the truth.

White men going to the Black man's house having sex with his wife would go on for years and still in some areas of Mississippi. The white man feeling grateful for good sex gives the Black man his very own pickup truck as a token for not killing him for fucking his wife. He then buys himself a new pickup truck and the cycle continues. Now, the Black man's status has changed in the Black culture. I did not say community because it is not a community, it is a slave culture. He can now ride around in a truck given to him for acting like a good nigger.

THE SEPARATE BUT EQUAL DOCTRINE

To become a citizen at birth, you must first be born in the US or certain territories belonging to the US such as Puerto Rico. They are subject to the jurisdiction of the United States. A person must have a parent or parents who were citizens at the time of birth. If you were born outside the US, you must meet these requirements outlined by the US Department of State. The Immigration and Nationality Act (INA) explains;

Naturalization is the process by which US citizenship is granted to a lawful permanent resident after meeting these requirements: Be a Lawful Permanent Resident of 5 Years, be Married to a US Citizen, Served in the US Military, or be a Child of a US Citizen[3]

Everything we did back then was separate from white people. When Muddear took me to the dentist, we walked towards the waiting room where white people sat. Instead of staying there, I remember us bypassing the waiting room and going along the side of the building. We entered through the back door into a dingy, messy room where the dentist came in to provide his services. Although I don't remember the dentist himself being a bigot, the difference in treatment between us and the whites set the mood of second-class citizenship.

During the 1920s until 1970, Black and White public appearance was separate but considered equal. Restaurants, shopping centers, and medical facilities were all separated. My mother took me to see a dentist, we walked towards the waiting room where white people sat but we couldn't go in that way. We entered through the back door into a dingy room where the dentist came in to provide dental services. Although I don't remember this

---

[3] https://www.usa.gov/become-us-citizen (Oct. 2021) US Citizenship for People Born Abroad or in US Territories

dentist being a bigot, the stark difference in the treatment between us and the whites stamped the Black race with a badge of inferiority.

According to PBS's *The First 100 Years* show on the Supreme Court, Homer Adolph Plessy was the plaintiff in a case to test the separate but equal law's constitutionality (Ferguson 1896. PBS). On June 7, 1892, Plessy bought a ticket on a train from New Orleans to Covington, Louisiana. He boarded the train and took a vacant seat in the whites-only car. Mr. Plessy refused to leave the car at the conductor's request, afterwards, his arrest and jailing came quickly.

The case of *Plessy v. Ferguson's* aim was to change a law passed in Louisiana in 1890 providing for separate railway carriages for the white and colored races. It stipulated that all passenger railways had to provide separate cars, which in theory, had supposed equal facilities. Convicted by a New Orleans court of violating the 1890 law, Plessy filed a petition against the presiding judge, Hon. John H. Ferguson. By claiming that the law violated the Equal Protection Clause of the 14th Amendment, he moved forward.

On May 18, 1896, the Supreme Court ruled on Plessy v. Ferguson declaring separate but equal on railroads. The protections of the 14th Amendment applied only to political and civil rights, not "social rights." Plessy lost the Supreme Court case thus setting the tone for Jim Crow actions towards Blacks by the White Population.

School Segregation in Mississippi

In 1954, Brown v. Board determined that racial segregation in schools was unconstitutional. This landmark court case set educational desegregation in motion. Around this time, Inverness had two elementary schools: one for whites called Central Delta Academy and the other one for everyone else. The Chinese and Jewish people who lived on the white side of town could also attend the white school, but Blacks could not.

The white folks who founded Central Delta Academy made it a private school. This allowed the school to operate from 1922 to 2010 without allowing a single Black student to attend classes. Finally, on May 21, 2010, it closed in defiance of the desegregation laws. The building went up for auction immediately and was demolished later that year.

Looking at the pictures, you can see that the school was well-maintained at the time of demolition. Many people tried to save the property and failed. The school would be for whites only or it wouldn't exist at all. Blacks would never sit in the chairs of the Inverness Central Delta Academy.

Racial Integrity Act of 1924
Black and white people did not mix under any circumstances. Back then, Blacks were paralyzed with a fear of white people. You see, in Mississippi, Black people are born to fail. It all starts on the birth certificate which labels us as "colored." We have no race, no ethnicity, no nationality; we are just "colored."

The word "colored" originates from the Racial Integrity Act of 1924, which is sometimes referred to as the Paper Genocide of Black America. This law criminalized interracial marriage and required that birth certificates record race as either "white" or "colored."

Charles Darwin and Walter Plecker created it to erase the heritage of Blacks and Native Indians. Darwin and Plecker knew that, if they could prove their heritage, the Blacks and Indians could eventually reclaim the lands that the whites had taken.

Plecker was proud of the law and his role in creating it. It was, he said, "the most perfect expression of the white ideal, and the most important ecumenical effort that has been made in 4,000 years." The act did not just make Blacks in Virginia second-class citizens, it also erased any acknowledgment of Indians. He claimed that the Indians no longer existed in the commonwealth. With a stroke of a pen, Virginia was on a path to eliminating the heritage of the following native groups: the Pamunkey Tribe, the Mattaponi Tribe, the Chickahominy Tribe, the Monacan Tribe, the Rappahannock Tribe, and the Nansemond Tribe among others4.

The systematic destruction of the Black race leaves us with heritage or lineage to build on. Our history simply perishes. Proverbs 29:18 states, "Where there is no vision, the people perish: but he that keepeth the law, happy is he." The race with nothing to look towards and nothing to look back on has no vision. This is how they made the Black man disappear from the American dream. After suffering for five hundred years, it is time Blacks and Indians stand up and fight!

No Opportunity for the Mississippi Black Man

Inverness is a plantation town with poor Black people born looking for a way out of the cotton fields. Mississippi had few choices for a Black man in 1967. He could chop cotton for five to six dollars a day, pick cucumbers for a dollar a day, or walk the streets of the Mississippi Delta with nothing to do.

---

4 Heim, Joe. *How a Long-Dead White Supremacist Still Threatens the Future of Virginia's Indian Tribe.* June 2015.

Being born Black in Mississippi is like being born a dog with a heavy chain around his neck. There is no future unless you carve it out for yourself. You are born into a breeding tank to populate the plantations as far as the eyes can see. As soon as you are old enough to play with it, the first toy you receive is a tractor, sometimes given to you by the white man. When the white man comes into your house, he never knocks; he just walks right in. I hated the Mississippi white man because of the life I experienced as a Mississippi Black man.

Three Types of Black Invernians

There are three categories of Black people living in Inverness. Each kind brings different qualities to our community.

First, some Black people settled there in the original Duncan Quarters (east of Highway 49) a long time ago. My grandmother, Mama Coon, and Uncle Nigga were originally from Duncan Quarters. I lived there with my family for a while.

Second, there are the Black people who were born and raised for generations on Bobby Duncan's and other plantations. Some of them still live on the plantation.

Third, there are plantation Blacks who moved to the town of Inverness. It was hard for them to assimilate into the neighborhood because it seemed as though they were out of place sometimes. They behaved in strange ways, such as having toilet bowls in the front yard.

Chinese and Jewish Shop Owners in Inverness

The Chinese loved the white man, but the white man left them alone and treated them as if they were invisible. The Chinese lived in the middle of the whites and the Blacks. They stayed to themselves and attended the white schools without problems. Because of this, they thought themselves to be on the same level as whites in the hierarchy.

The Chinese wanted our money but still held up their noses at the Blacks when we came into their stores. They would jump to serve whites and ignore Blacks until the white folks walked out the door. I could never figure out how they made their way to Inverness and opened grocery stores. The only Black-owned store in town was Limmy Walker, across from the school. He had a store full of junk food for the kids.

Once desegregation took over the state of Mississippi, Blacks started to buy new clothes from the Jews. There was a store in town owned by a Jewish man named Abraham. He profited off of our community, and we let it happen. Abraham sold classy clothing--shoes, slacks, shirts, and more—to the Invernians. Abraham sold so much stuff to our people that he made enough money to move out of Inverness to Downtown Indianola. He moved into the closed movie theater and converted it into a department store.

Downtown Indianola

That movie theater brings back memories of *The Night of the Living Dead*, which came out in October 1968. The horror of that movie possessed me as I watched it. For the next twenty years or so, the thought of it still scared me. That's right, *The Night of the Living Dead* put the fear of God in me. It was my first time going to the movies. I remember so vividly, walking to the box office, getting a ticket, and going back outside around to the stairs that led up to the balcony. Blacks had to watch movies from the second-floor balcony, separate from the whites who were on the ground floor. I never got to see a movie from the ground floor in Indianola.

Downtown Indianola was the big city in my eyes. Every Saturday morning, people from Inverness went to Indianola and Greenville for shopping. We went to Piggly Wiggly, the most popular grocery store at the time, and, of course, to Abraham's department store.

After the daytime shopping, we started nighttime clubbing. In Inverness, there was Fannie Mae's Café, which we called "Ludie's," and it was always packed on Friday and Saturday nights. There was also Adam's, Hookey's, Jim's, Walter B's, and Cats Place. Indianola had Club Ebony, owned by the Sheppard and later by B. B. King, the White Rose, and the 308 Club.

We had record hop after record hop and sometimes there were two or three going on at one time. Mink Eye was a DJ from the country. He had the big speakers that made your ears ring for days. It seemed like people wanted the music up as loud as it would go. Mink Eye ended up marrying my sister, Joyce Ann.

When I found out my sister had married a Stuckey, I said "Damn Sam!" We did not get along as families, but we had to squash that squabble when they jumped the broom.

The Inverness Gang

One night while looking for cigarettes, Big Mike, Fat Punk, Poor Hunkey, and I slipped over to the white side of town. When a truck approached, we hid in the tree line and waited for someone to throw a cigarette butt out the window. When it happened, Poor Hunkey could not wait until the truck was out of sight. He darted out to get the butt, and the people in the truck saw him. The brake lights lit up, and the truck started backing up. We started running and escaped before the truck got to us. Poor Hunkey still had the butt, so we all satisfied ourselves with a puff.

These are the fellows who ran with the Inverness Gang:

Big Mike, being true to his nickname, was a big dude. He acted as the equalizer among the group of hoodlums we ran with. When people saw us, they feared us mostly because of Big Mike. But, in reality, Poor Hunkey was the one who brought the pain. Big Mike played high school football and was a force to be reckoned with both on and off the field. He was a tackle for the Gentry Rams and was on his way to getting a fat scholarship if he could survive the four years of high school football. Unfortunately, his football career did not make it past the tenth grade. During a muddy game in Gentry, he tore the ligaments in his knee. Man, we were behind him all the way, and so was the team.

Fat Punk's nickname stuck with him, even though he wasn't gay. He was tall, solid, and heavy for his age. His dad was Mr.

Tommy Strangler who, in my opinion, was the most feared Black man in Inverness. Fat Punk had about ten brothers and three sisters. The Stranglers were the largest family in town.

Sammy was my best friend for life. I could trust this person on every level, and I did. He had my back when no one else would. When he got his paychecks from working for Mr. Billy Ed, he would share some of the money with me. That is how good of a friend he was. Sammy was the best!

Willie D. was the weird one of the bunch. He always came up with the strangest thing to do and eat. After he learned how to kill robins with a rock, he taught the rest of us. Willie D. had us all climbing up in the seed house, playing around in the cotton seeds after they had been semi-cleaned.

Huh Huh (whose real name was Lester) was one of the Brooks brothers. We called him Huh Huh because of the way he talked. I cannot figure out a way to describe the way he sounds, but it was just weird. Huh Huh had one brother called Big Lip and another called Headquarters. Big Head David was another name for Headquarters because his head was huge. He probably wore a seven or eight and a half hat. He always had his head leaning to the left for some reason.

On the other side of town was my cousin Perry who ran with Hezzie Lee, Terry, Vernon, Richard, Dee, and Donald Lee. Although we ran on separate turfs, we were always friendly to each other.

This group of baby criminals broke into Inverness Elementary School at least once a month. Sammy went in through one of the classroom's open windows and let the rest of us in through the door. The first stop was always the teachers' lounge where we would rummage and pillage. We found feminine products to toss around and made fun of who they may belong to.

After we tore up the classrooms and the teachers' lounge, we'd usually cook something to eat. In the kitchen, we were afraid to stand up all the way because Mr. Limmy could see the kitchen window from his house. So, we duck walked around the kitchen and set up a pot to boil hotdogs and sausages. We took the cooked links to the stage, set up a hot dog banquet, and left the mess there. In retrospect, I am a little bit disappointed in my behavior back then.

King of the Toxic Hill

There are train tracks right across the street from Downtown Inverness. The train would stop sometimes to unload this white, poisonous substance used in the cotton fields. When the train left, the white substance was just in reach of us so that we could play in it. It was probably lime or some kind of weed killer used on the fields.

They unloaded this toxin on the Black side of town, again poisoning our kids. People for the Black side of town would take a bucket of the stuff to put in the vegetable gardens, and no one ever said a word about it. As a little kid, the mound of powder stacked two stories high presented a great opportunity to go mountain climbing.

There was a border dividing the town that separated the whites and Blacks. I lived close to the border around the age of eight. Some white boys my age lived across the imaginary line, so sometimes we would "accidentally" play together on the lime mountains. One time, while I was playing king of the hill alone, two white boys came over and wanted me to get off the piles so that they could play on them. I refused to move and invited them to take the hill from me. They tried and tried to throw me off but could not. Lucky me, I threw both of them off the top of the lime mountain many times, making me king for the day.

THE FAMILY

Grandpa Bud and Mama Coon

I did not meet my grandfather on my mother's side until he was ninety-four years old. He left the Delta way before I was born under a directive from a white man.

Here is his story as I recall it. Perry "Bud" Smith was born in 1897 on a plantation southeast of Inverness. He was a sharecropper. This means that, in exchange for an unreasonable percentage of the profit, the white man would give him the seeds and land needed to grow crops. This was a widely practiced process in the Mississippi Delta.

For many years, this process worked well for my grandpa. That is until the white landowner died, and his son took over. The son was a mean and surly white boy whom Bud had to show respect to, not because he deserved it, but because he was white. One year after the harvest, the son short-changed my grandpa out of $3,000. When Bud asked for the withheld monies, the son told him that he had twenty-four hours to get off the land.

My grandfather had a family: his wife, Mama Coon (whose real name was Willie Ann Robinson), and his daughter, Genella Robinson. He divided his $2,000 profit between him and Mama Coon, left Mississippi, and headed to Chicago. Mama Coon later moved to Inverness and bought a house in Duncan Quarters.

Duncan Quarter got its name from the cotton gin owner, Bobby Duncan. It was a Black suburban area on the southeast side of town. My mother, her sister, and her brother were born and raised there. Duncan Quarters was shabby and close to the town's garbage dump.

When Blacks moved from the plantations, they had the opportunity to live in the area where the garbage dump stood for years, and they took it. Anywhere was better than living on the plantation. I can remember going across this narrow wood plank bridge and over a sewage stream to get to my grandma's house. Believe it or not, in 2018, Black people still live in Duncan Quarters.

Southern Black Cuisine

Our grandparents lived to be in their eighties and nineties because, back then, food was not pumped full of chemicals. The animals we'd eat, mostly hogs and chickens, grew up in the backyard. It was a simple life with everything we needed right there. There were no Walmart or dollar stores. The women cooked every day while the men went to the cotton and soybean fields. We always had something on the table—neck bones, ham hocks, chicken, or pork. I can honestly say that I never went hungry and I never went dirty.

We grew up eating chitterlings, the intestines of a hog, which Black southerners consider to be a delicacy. We also eat the pig's feet, tail, ears, jaw, and other organs. If a Black kid eats like this, he hardly ever needs a doctor's care because he grows up strong.

My family ate parts of the chicken the dog would not eat. Us kids ate the gizzards, wings, backs, feet, and necks while the older ones enjoyed the breasts and thighs. If a Black person tells you they are from the Delta, rest assured they grew up on this type of comfort food.

A Childhood Experiment

On a hot summer day when I was nine years old, my curiosity consumed me. I wanted to know how a cardboard box would hold up if I built a fire inside of it. So, I found a beer box, went under the house, and started my experiment. I made the box into a stove by cutting a door on one side of the box. Muddear usually bought deli meats and cheeses by the slice wrapped in white butcher paper from the Chinese stores. I took some of the paper from the fridge and went under the house with the box, the paper, and some big kitchen matches.

After getting everything set up, I went to find Tenia, my sister, so that she could witness my incredible experiment. When we had everything together, I lit a match and tried to light the paper, but it blew out several times. In hindsight, I should have known better, but

I lit another match the same thing happened. Finally, the third match stayed lit.

When the butcher paper caught fire, my sister took off like a rocket and left me to deal with the fire under the house. Not knowing that air would make it worse, I kept trying to blow it out and failed. By that time, I decided to get out from under the house. Since we had chickens in the yard, there was a pot with a handle sitting there under the spigot full of water. I grabbed it and, in a panic, I threw the water against the side of the house.

The water didn't extinguish the flame and the box caught fire. I started crawling back up under the house when my brother, Wes, grabbed my legs and pulled me out. I often imagine what would have happened if I made it back under the house. Wes took his time hooking up the water hose and turning it towards the fire. Soon the flame was out, and I started worrying about Muddear whooping my behind. I was nine years old when I took my last whooping. After that, I was a good boy around town. I didn't get into any trouble that Muddear would hear about.

Gettin' High Before Shop Class

All the boys from Inverness would come together whenever they could—on the bus ride to and from school, during breaks and lunch, and even walking back home from the bus after school. We smoked weed almost every day behind the gym. I never understood why no teacher ever checked us for smoking weed. After we smoked, we went back to shop class where Mr. Smith made us work hard on our projects. He knew we were high but did not bother with it.

Mr. Smith was a Black rancher who owned many acres of land. From him, I learned how to grow gardens, plant shrubs, do landscaping. And unfortunately, drive tractors. We traveled to many cities in Mississippi fixing up people's yards and working on his plantation in Belzoni. Most of us were Future Plantations of America members with the blue corduroy jacket. In shop class with

Mr. Smith, we also learned how to weld and the many facets of agribusiness.

Family Life

Inverness, Mississippi is a modern-day plantation-based plantation town located east of the Mississippi River, just eight miles south of the Sunflower River off United States Highway 49. The home of famous blues singer Little Milton Campbell and neighboring town to Indianola, where B.B. King, another blues singer, left on his road to stardom. Lil' Milton, named after his father, had a bunch of brothers; I remember Bill, Johnny, LA, London, and Joe. The only sister I remember is Doll. Other significant family names in and of Inverness are Stapleton, Denton, Sibley, Hayes, Langston, Thomas, Price, White, Robinson, Strangler, Lockhart, Herring, and of course the Smiths. Other names came directly from the plantations like the Stuckeys, Spiveys, and the Zollycaufers.

It does not take much effort to know which part of town a person came from; one could tell by the way they dressed. The plantation folks were a little tougher and sometimes dusty; not to say they weren't good people—they literally worked hard. Johnnie McPherson was my best friend and from the country. They were always rivals with the town folks; every Saturday night, one could always count on a good fight between the country boys and town folk.

My oldest brother Tho, better known as Theodore Ricks, was the leader of the pack when it came to starting and winning fights with the plantation folks. He was a real gangster around town harassing everyone who thought they were "cool." On one occasion, I saw him grab a man by the top of his jeans—in the center of the man's back—dragging him around the bar like a rag doll without remorse.

The man kept saying, "Let me go Theotha, Theotha, let me go!" My brother would not let him go until he was thoroughly embarrassed.

One day, I must have angered my older brother badly. I had a smart mouth, but I cannot remember what exactly I said to him. He lifted me with both hands around my neck, I could not breathe, and my feet were dangling. Tenia, my middle sister was in the yard twirling a baton.

Tenia yelled at Tho, "Let him go!"

He did not stop choking me, so she hit him across the head with her baton, and he dropped me and left home for a while. I do not remember what happened afterward.

The Po Po's had no problem watching Black people fight but when the fight ended, they would come in and take the losers to jail. I watched my brother kick a dude with such style it looked like it was out of a Bruce Lee movie! He squatted down to the floor and all I saw was one foot and leg going straight towards this person's head. Ka-POW! Upside the head and the dude hit the floor. Only two licks passed; my brother's roundhouse and his opponent hitting the floor!

We were not poor but if we were, I did not know it. I lived on peanut butter and jelly sandwiches, salmon croquettes, biscuits, and syrup. Other meals we used to eat included grilled cheese sandwiches made with government cheese. This is the best cheese a man could ever eat, maybe it's nostalgia, but that was some damn good cheese. We had cereal with carnation milk and water and white bread sandwiches with mayonnaise, ketchup, or sugar to eat. These were the staples we had no choice but to grow on.

The old highway 49 used to run straight through Inverness. After the white folks decided a new highway going through Inverness would be bad for business, the State routed the highway around the city. Inverness dying a slow death in the wake of not receiving new business, new residence, or new traffic to support the town—seemed inevitable. They did this because they were afraid of the Black people leaving town or moving off the plantation to live in Inverness.

Let me explain. Inverness is/was a cotton-ginning and plantation working town. All cotton from a fifty-mile radius in either direction came to Duncan's Cotton Gin Company for processing. During the harvest season, every Black male sixteen or older worked for Bobby Duncan at the Inverness cotton gin. The Inverness men were usually employed at the cotton gin year-round.

The plantation folks picked, planted, nurtured, and transported the cotton to the gin in Inverness. They had a great system of capitalizing on the Black race for cotton ginning. The gin ran twenty-four hours a day and seven days a week during the fall cotton season. Bobby Duncan expected Blacks to work every day of the week for as little as seven dollars an hour. Back then, that was good pay, at least they thought it was.

Blacks living in Inverness had long experience in working cotton and soybeans on the plantations. The white man built row houses and gave them to Blacks for rent. As long as they worked the fields, they could live in the row house. The houses were sometimes called shotgun houses because you could see through the front door and out the back. These row houses were always in disrepair; most people who lived in the row houses would not try to fix them up and I understood why. The white man never paid enough money to make any repairs, nor did the white property owner make any repairs so why would the Black man do it?

Out the back door, was a little four by four feet room built like a one-room shack with a little design cutout on the door. This was the bathroom; better known as the "outhouse." There was a three to five feet hole to collect the shit. When it filled up, we would just slide the outhouse over another hole. Once the hole was open for a reasonable amount of time, the entire house shifted to a freshly dug hole where convenient. Inside the outhouse was a toilet seat attached to a board to sit on. If you were part of the field hands, you squatted straight to the ground. Newspapers, magazines, old clothing, or whatever you could get to clean your behind would work for wiping.

Our neighborhood was always somewhere near the cotton fields. Never could understand why we were near a cotton field or a garbage dump. In Inverness, our neighborhood was near both; in

Indianola, only near the garbage dump. This design was most likely done on purpose.

My family, whom I love dearly, consists of halves; two half-brothers and two half-sisters. Some people may not know what that means. For us, it only means that each of the children has different fathers but the same mother. On our birth certificate, colored is our race.

I was born July 31, 1959, in Isola, about three miles south of Inverness. The doctor even felt it hard to call me human. I later found out that the occasion of my birth was a nuisance to the doctor. Interrupting his dinner to deliver a Black baby was just too much. My parents went to the back door of his house and asked for help with the delivery. The choice is to call me "colored" or call me a nigger. All I remember is the banana box filling in as my crib. My banana box remains on the bar at Cat's place. What a way to enter the world!

Our family of halves includes Theodore, who's the oldest. A proud and tough Vietnam Veteran who came back damaged from the war. Theodore was better known as "Tho" by the community and my other brother Wesley, better known as Wes. My two sisters are Joyce and Tenia. I had another couple of half-brothers named George after my father and the other was Jerry. Not to list Black babies' father's names on the birth certificate was a cover-up to start. My family was all half-brothers and sisters.

The Historic Inverness Tornado

Three Tornados hit Inverness on February 21, 1971. One would be a deadly historic F-5 monster. That day, I was a twelve-year-old doing twelve-year-old things. Curtis and I had built a go-cart out of scrap plywood, broomsticks, and some old tires we found around the town. It was his time to push so I rode the kart through and behind the cotton gin, in the area we were not supposed to travel through. Curtis pushed me to my mother's house where we drove to the front yard. Just as we made it there, it started to rain or should

I say drizzle a little bit, so we put the go-cart on the porch for the evening.

Man, we were hungry, so we went into the house to the kitchen and found something to eat. All Black people in Inverness had a log roll of bologna where a perfectly cut hunk or slice to eat raw or fried—satisfied any hunger. That day, we were so hungry the plan was to eat it raw. Before making go-kart plans, we had to check the weather, so we went outside to see if it had started to rain. The clouds were heavy and dark but produced no rain. All the elements of a storm presented themselves, so we decided to put the go-kart on the porch out of harm's way.

Hungry, we went back into the house and found that big red bologna log. With a good knife, we cut it over the kitchen sink, serving up two good thick slices of bologna. By that time, the rain had started to come down and I could see the raindrops on the kitchen window over the sink. Paying the rain no mind, I sawed another slice off the two-foot bologna log.

About halfway through the slice, a 2 x 4 board slammed into the kitchen window shattering the glass. Curtis immediately started laughing at the shocking moment. By that time, I had finished cutting my slice and held it in my hand. Either I dropped the knife in the kitchen sink or on the floor, I am not sure where it went in those moments. I do know I held on to my slice of bologna before, during, and after the storm came through.

The wind was high and the rain came fast, feeling like a sandblaster on my face and hands.

I yelled to Curtis, "Stop laughing and get under the table," by that time he stopped laughing and was diving for the floor under the table.

With bologna in hand, I went under a chair. I was small enough to fit under there far enough to protect me from the gritty sting of the tornado's wind and rain.

Out of nowhere, Brenda, a friend of my sister, grabbed me and threw me from under the chair, and immediately jumped in my spot. Without hesitation, I grabbed her by the hair and pulled her out of my way, and just about fell back into my spot. All the while, the wind and rain sound like a freight train pummeled my face. Seems like the time went in slow motion for the next five minutes or so.

I peeped around the corner and saw my sister trying to hold the front door. The wind was so powerful that the top of the door and the bottom of the door had bent inward from the force. She held the door and was screaming all at the same time getting sprinkled with the debris carried by the wind and rain.

My brother yelled at her saying, "Let that door go!"

Letting it go, she ran to get under the bed.

She didn't make it. About a foot away, a wall fell on her trapping her underneath.

The wind and rain were still coming in hard. I tried to cover my face and hold on to my bologna at the same time. When I looked at it, so much of the grain and sand had lodged in the bologna slice, so I let it go.

As I think back on that day, Curtis was about to go home and my sister told him to wait until the rain stopped before he left so he stayed, probably saving his life. After the wind stopped, we found that there had been three tornados that day to touch down in Inverness. The house was in shambles, totaled with the roof was gone, walls in halves—a complete mess.

I looked up from under the chair and saw my brother Wes bleeding from the face and neck. He had a three-inch gash in his neck and acted like he was a tough man; I guess at that time he was.

My sister was yelling under the rubble when my oldest brother showed up to rescue her.

He was slinging rubble and saying, "I'm gone get you Tenia, I'm gonna get you Tenia," until he finally got to her.

I remember him carrying her to my grandmother's. She was all right though, only a nail in the knee and scared.

My other sister Joyce came from the back room with her book in hand but no injuries. Curtis, Brenda, and I were fine, but noticing the extreme damage the tornado did to the Jim Walters home left us in awe of nature's fury. The roof was gone and stuff was everywhere. It was quite an ordeal. A lot of people died that day, but not us.

Moving Around After the Inverness Tornadoes

I remember the first time my family moved. It was right after three tornadoes hit Inverness on February 21, 1971, at 6:00 pm. After the tornados hit, the sheriff's department thought that people would be coming into the city to steal, so they blocked all entrances and exits. They would only allow recovery vehicles to enter the city.

I commend my dad, George Reed, for thinking outside the box. His friend, Mr. Dillion, was a mortician who owned a funeral home in Indianola, so he borrowed his hearse for the trip to Inverness. Mr. Dillion was also my math teacher at Inverness Elementary School.

All of us—my mother, brother, and sisters—loaded up in the hearse for the trip out of Inverness. For the next three days, we stayed at the Travelodge Hotel near the crossroads of Highway 49 and Highway 82. Then, we were blessed with a house in South Gate three days after the storm. South Gate was a brand-new subdivision on the south end of Indianola.

The first house at the end of this chapter was 137 Ethel Waters Drive. It later became the home directly in front of Little Milton Campbell's family. There was Bill, Johnnie, LA, London, Joe, and Doll Campbell. We were all from Inverness so it was just like home, except for the school.

London and LA became my best friends. LA was on the same baseball team as me. Looking back, I think that LA kept me going when I thought I wanted to quit baseball. London, on the other hand, used to try and fight me after school almost every day. He was a couple of years older than me, and I think he was a little bit jealous that I was on a baseball team. The coach, Benny Parker, was a great guy. He gave me the opportunity to learn about baseball. I was the starting second baseman, and I was pretty good! Po-Bone, whose real name was Carl Williams, was the pitcher. He became one of my best friends at Carver Elementary School.

Muddear did not like the living conditions in South Gate, so we left there pretty damn quick. Moving back to Inverness came with many changes, but there was an advantage. I had gotten to know many people in Indianola so, when we were bussed there for high school, I already knew many of my classmates.

Back in Inverness, we were living in the back of my grandmother's house, which is pictured in the middle photo.

That was the second house we lived in after the tornadoes. My mother struck a deal with the tornado relief workers. They promised to repair my grandmother's house for free as long as they could live there while they assisted in the recovery efforts.

Then, we moved again. We lived in the third house for about a year, across the street from a man named Dr. Johnson. He was a faith healer with a church in Drew, Mississippi. People say this man could take away any pain and bless you with riches if you believed.

Living in the house with Dr. Johnson, were Billy Ray, Kathy, Naomi, and Idell. They were all good friends of mine while living at 109 Quick Circle Drive. Other friends on the same street are Martha, Sam, C. W., and, Willie Ed. Ross lived two houses down from me. I cannot forget Kill Roy, another good friend of mine.

Goodtimes and Trouble the Inverness Way

When I was about eight or nine, I hung out with my then-best friend Curtis White. One day while running around town and playing hard in the sun, we decided to go walking on the edge of the white side and Black side of town. We were heading in the direction of highway 49 with the hardware store across the street on the left and Billy Ed's on the left corner of highway 49 and Third Street. There was one more gas station on the corner across from Billy Ed's; they sold candy and other junk food more especially Now and Later candy.

Curtis and I, went inside the gas station to buy some of those Now and Laters. The store owner had hundreds of packs on display just for the taking. There were lots of them on the counter looking very good to eat. The packages were nice looking and lined up the right dress, I couldn't stand the temptation. With only a nickel in my pocket, I bought one pack of Now and Later for me and Curtis bought one pack as well.

Just about the time I gave the white man my nickel for the Now and Later a car pulled up needing services so Mr. white man hurriedly went outside. He left me and Curtis in the store with all those now laters on the counter looking at me.

I said to Curtis, "Don't take any of the candy, it looks too organized and it could be a trap; I will take an extra package of candy and we can share/split them on the way home."

He said, "OK."

I looked around and did not see anyone else in the store/gas station. With that assurance, I grabbed two packs of now and laters from the boxes, and said to Curtis, let's go partner.

We left the gas station heading back from where we came. About a few hundred feet from the gas station, we heard someone yelling, "Hey boys," so we tried to ignore the noise, but he just yelled louder.

I said to Curtis, "Did you take a pack of Now and Later?"

He said, "Yeah, I took one just like you did!"

I replied, "Damn Curtis, now we are busted for taking too many now and laters, you should have listened to me. I knew if we took too many candies from the boxes, we would get busted for stealing them. So now, we have a decision to make, run or go see what the gas station man wants?"

We decided to go back to the station and face the penalty of stealing. I said to Curtis, through the extra packages of now or later under that old car so when we get back to the white man, we would only have one pack. We threw the extras under the car and went to see what he wanted. He grabbed me by the arm and Curtis by the collar then took us back into the station and stood us up against the wall. We stood there like ornaments on the wall waiting for the man to say something.

He stared at us and said, "I ought to take you niggers out to a tree and hang the both of you!"

Not scared and not saying a word, waiting for a break to run or get away. We stood firm and waited for the outcome. I was thinking about how I was going to get away from this white man. He then called the police and within a few minutes, Mr. Otis appeared in his old white Galaxy 500 Ford. Mr. Otis was a big fat white man with a huge drooping belly; he walked slowly with a distinct 30-inch gait. He came into the office of the gas station, took a look at us, and pointed to his car. Curtis and I hurried to the car to get away from the hanging man.

I knew we were on our way to the slammer but to my surprise, he took us to my grandmother's house and turned us over to her. My grandmother, Mama Coon, ran a bordello all week long. People came there to buy liquor, listen to the latest blues and buy time with women for sexual favors. Occasionally, I would ease my way in there doing the dog; people would give me a quarter or two for my troubles. I have even crept down the hallway and peeped through the keyhole for some eye candy.

Since it was only Now and Later candies, I went up to Billie Ed's gas station on almost a daily basis to work off my punishment. One would be curious about that because Billy Ed is a white man and my Uncle Roosevelt had a gas station on the other corner. I just could not get myself to go to my uncle's station. Maybe it was because I wanted to own that gas station. I had a dream about it at the age of seven and I was obsessed with my Muddear buying or even renting it.

Anyway, back to Billie Ed's! I would go there and hang around hoping the man would give me a job, but he never did. Mr. Yank was Sammy's daddy; he worked as a gas attendant for Billie Ed. I watched that man go into action when a car pulled up to the pumps. He had energy and moved fast, cleaning the windshield, checking the oil, tires, and wiper blades. He would tell the driver to pop the hood so he could check the oil. With the hood opened, Mr. Yank would pull a dirty oil-stained rag from his pocket, and at the same time, he pulled out the oil dipstick to check the level.

I could not help but notice how he reacted to a car driven by white folks as opposed to a car driven by Black folks. He was remarkably not that interested in the welfare of the Black-owned automobile. I really could not blame him though; I am sure he had instructions to stay focused on the white-owned vehicles.

Remember, this man could balance a tire like no other; Mr. Yank had an amazing touch when it came to mechanics!

Racing and Facing Adulthood: The Inverness Way

One of my best memories about lording around Billie Ed's Gas Station was the Coon Hunting Mules. Once or twice a month, Sammy, Mike, and I would go to the corral to saddle up the mules. Sammy rode Emma, Mike rode Possum and I rode Trigger. I had an old army saddle with the split in the middle and it was ideal for how I rode the Trigger. Mike seems to have the hardest time from saddling up to getting knocked off going under a tree. Sammy was the daredevil; he rode Trigger like the lone ranger, fast and hard all the time. He was the best rider and could make that mule, Emma do anything.

One day while racing down a street in Inverness, I had Trigger wide open as we approached the end of the street. Trigger refused to slow down, so here I am approaching a hard left turn running at about thirty miles an hour. I snatched up hard on the reins a few times getting harder each time. Finally, Trigger stopped instantly and started to slide on the asphalt road. After about thirty feet of sliding, the front feet went forward and the back feet went backward. Before you knew it, Trigger's bell was sliding on the asphalt road while my feet were up by her ears.

When it was all over, Trigger had bruises on all four legs and her belly. The scratch was nothing serious; it looked like a superficial wound. I went uptown and bought some ointment to put on the scratches. We took the mules to the woods south of Inverness regularly. Riding Trigger was one of my best releases growing up in Inverness, a deprived area of the Mississippi Delta. Adulthood would come knocking on my door soon enough, but there were some great times had even with the clouds of racism persistent in our Mississippi skies.

Military day at Gentry High School was a great day for me. At that time, I decided to become a Marine. Not sure if it is because my older brother had joined the Marines a few years earlier or was it the pure sense of adventure I had at the time. Nevertheless, I went to the recruiting station all pumped up to be a marine, just to be deflated because of a minor technicality.

The Marine recruiter started to make me comfortable by offering coffee, water sodas, and chips. This stuff was free so naturally, I took all I could get my hands on. I'm feeling pretty laid back and at home in the recruiting station now, so yes, I got comfortable. Now, it is time to start the drill, asking questions to disqualify my application for the Marines.

"Have you ever been injured?"

"No."

"Do you have asthma?"

"No."

"Do you smoke marijuana?"

"Hell yeah! All the time!"

Well damn, that was the nail in the coffin with my journey for the Marines.

The recruiter said, "Sorry Mr. Smith, we can't take you on account of your marijuana use."

"What? This is my life you have just ended! I cannot stay in Mississippi, and you will need to help me do something to get me out of here. I am not a tractor driver; I can't pick cucumbers nor can I work for the plantation owners. Can you please do something to help me?" I asked.

He said, "Wait just a minute," as he stood up in the crisp uniform that I will never wear and walked out of the room.

A few minutes later he returned and said, "Come with me."

We walked down the hall, took a left, and a right into the Army's recruiting office. The Marine recruiter introduced me to the Army recruiter and asked him to take care of me. I'm starting to feel proud again, I still have a way out with them knowing I smoke marijuana. I joined the Army that day, at the age of seventeen while still in high school under the Delayed Entry Program (DEP). I still need a parent's signature though.

My senior year in high school, I ended up flunking my twelfth-grade English class with Mrs. Shortridge. She caused me to spend my summer in summer school. It was not her fault that I did not make the grade. I knew I had to graduate or risk the chance of not going to the Army. During that year, I was attempting to work at the cotton gin where I had to push the bales of cotton up the ramp. By the end of the summer, I passed my English class.

I did not attend the Prom or the class of the 1977 Gentry High School graduation ceremony. I just could not find the energy to go through these public spectacle ceremonies. I did have some social engagements, but none that I can remember. After high school, I thought I was the cool smart guy who knew everything. I left Inverness on a Greyhound bus on August 26, 1977, heading to Jackson, Mississippi to be inducted into the United States Army.

Young Love

Everyone has a story about a fling or a relationship experienced as a teenager. Mine began when I met a young woman by the name of Karen in the cotton fields of Mississippi. I immediately fell for this young woman. We liked each other and for the summer of 1977; we spent every possible moment together. I met her brothers and sisters, who numbered in the teens.

The journey from Inverness to Morehead, Mississippi was a challenge, but I wanted to see this woman so badly that I rode my twenty-inch bicycle down the highway every bit of ten miles round trip from Inverness to Morehead sometime twice a weekend.

Dorothy was Karen's older sister, and she was a sweetheart, later passing away from cancer at a very young age. I remember going to Morehead and spending the day at Dorothy's house. She always cooked, and I always ate there. The kitchen was my favorite spot. I loved her family, and they seemed to like me and Karen as a couple.

The moment came where it was time for me to ship off to the Army on August 26, 1977. With Karen there to see me off on the Greyhound, I told her I would be back. I needed to figure out what was in store for me joining the Army, so she agreed to wait for me. At that time, I had no idea that she was pregnant with my son.

Fort Knox

Boot camp was six weeks and Active Individual Training (AIT) was six months. I trained to be a diesel mechanic (63C10) capable of repairing tanks in a shop and the field—and I loved it. I was already prepared for boot camp when I arrived at Fort Knox, Kentucky. Fort Knox is the location of America's gold resources. It is a heavily fortified military base with a hundred thousand troops to protect it. I was stationed at the base from August 1977 through March 1978 for training.

I bought my first car while I was there—a 1973 Ford Gran Torino. I drove it back to the base just before Valentine's Day in 1978. It was a risk to have a car on the base because it made it so easy to get busted by the law for some nonsense.

I met a white boy, Johns, at boot camp, and we drove to his home in my car. He lived towards Louisville, outside of the city, about one hundred and fifty miles from base. Here's the bad part: we picked up an ounce of cocaine in Radcliff, Kentucky. I stuffed the ounce under the driver's seat, and we were off on our trip. Driving into the late night, we were almost there when we came to a fork in the road. Johns told me to take the fork on the right, so I was about to take it. Then he told me to take the fork on the left, so I swerved to make the left turn.

The highway patrol must have been following me the whole time because when I swerved, he put the lights on and pulled me over. Mind you, I'm a Black man, somewhere in redneck Kentucky in the middle of the night with an ounce of cocaine in the car.

The trooper immediately said, "Get out of the car!"

Johns exited the car with me, approached the officer, and said, "Sir, he is new to this area, and he's just trying to take me home. We are both soldiers at Fort Knox, and I asked him to bring me home for a family emergency. Can you please let us go?"

The officer shined his light on me, looking in my face to see if I looked scared or high, and then on to Johns.

He replied, "You had better keep that car on the road boy! Now get out of here!"

The officer let us go. That could have been a terrible experience and some jail time for sure.

There were three hills at Fort Knox: Misery, Agony, and Heartbreak. Every soldier that went through there will never forget them; we climbed these hills almost daily. Each and every day, it seemed like we were up and down those hills constantly.

I was getting ready to travel back to the Delta during an Active Individual Training (AIT) break. The plan was to travel south to Inverness. A couple of friends offered to pay for gas and help me drive. They were on their way further south to New Orleans. Both were Black men from Louisiana who happened to be my friends during boot camp and AIT. One had a nickname, "Mud Bone," and the other "Red." I never could remember their real names!

We made it to a Greyhound bus station in Indianola on Valentine's Day at four o'clock in the morning. The 1973 Gran Torino did a great job getting us there. We climbed the old worn steps up to the porch and went inside the station.

I was out front, so I went in first. At the counter, I saw the bell and rang it. Eerily enough, no one answered. So, I rang it again, still no answer. Mud Bone went over to the Coke machine and dropped a quarter in the slot. Then, the Coke machine's door swung open and, a bunch of change fell to the floor.

I yelled, in a very authoritarian voice, "Don't touch anything! Back up and out, let's go. Someone must have just robbed the place."

We eased our way back across the porch, down the creepy stairs, and into the car.

Red was in the back, Mud Bone had just sat down, and I had one foot in the driver seat when it happened. The Indianola Police had guns pointed at us like white on rice.

They said, "Freeze, get out of the car, and put your hands up!"

They took us to jail, booked us, and charged us with the robbery at the Indianola Bus Station. All this time, I professed our innocence. Back then, we were getting our military pay twice a month, so, we were three Black men with pockets full of money. We were guilty no matter what according to them.

The bus station in Indianola was a frequently robbed spot. Blacks would hold conversations about when was the best time to hit it.

Mud Bone and Red did not want to make a phone call about the arrest, but I did. I called Joyce, my sister, and asked her to call Muddear. Muddear called my dad, George, and he called in his Masonic Brothers. The Indianola Police unlocked the cell door and brought us to the front.

They said, "You are free to go after you pay the $35 jailing fee."

Mud Bone and Red agreed to pay the fine, but I refused.

I said, "I did not do anything wrong, so I am not going to pay."

To make a long story short, the Masons paid the fine and gave me the receipt. I kept that receipt for almost ten years. I intended to go back to Indianola with a lawyer, get the money back, and have the records removed. I finally lost the receipt and forgot about revenging the whole incident.

I left fort Knox and headed to Fort Bragg, North Carolina. There, my assignment was to Signal Battalion. I worked in the motor pool on wheeled vehicles like the Gamma Goat and the deuce and half truck. When I left fort Knox, I thought a job with the tanks was in the cards but ended up with wheeled vehicles. This was a good chance for me because now the Army had to train me on how to fix wheeled vehicles and generators. I was off to Fort Lee, Virginia for six weeks of training for my new job.

After about three years at Fort Bragg, I earned a promotion to Staff Sergeant; not without some hassle. There is this paper called the *Army Times*, published every month. In the paper, they list "cut-off scores." Cut-off scores indicate who is up for promotion by the accumulation of a higher number of points. So, if your accumulated points are greater than the points listed in the paper for that particular military occupational specialty (MOS), your promotion should come immediately.

Somehow, I made the score six months earlier and was not promoted. I found out that my lily-white commanders had deliberately hidden my promotion orders. They did not want me to be in charge of all the white buck sergeants so they hid my promotion orders. That was my first encounter with real racism in the Army. So, from this point in my military career onward—I watched everything and everybody to ensure it would never happen again.

Raising My Son

After spending eight months training at Fort Knox, I returned to Inverness to find that I had a son. Karen, the girl I loved as a teenager, named him WJ.

My first response was the baby was not mine. It really pissed me off that I was not told about the pregnancy until after the baby's birth. When information, or should I say when very significant information is withheld, it creates a level of doubt even when the truth is told. Sometimes this level of doubt cannot be reversed. Me being eighteen and not as educated, I felt that there was too much ambiguity about the pregnancy. Why would you hide such a thing if we're on good terms?

With this uncertainty, I could not bring myself back to trusting in the relationship again. Once my son was born, and there was no doubt that he was mine—as a new father, I stepped up to the plate to take care of my son. I knew I needed to do the right thing for my child, so I started to send money by way of Muddear.

Between Karen and I, there was no room for a marriage or even a relationship beyond us being good friends and taking care of our son. I was a soldier, so I was married to the Army. One drill sergeant told me, if the Army wanted me to have a wife, they would have issued me one. I believed I was the best damn soldier I could be at the time.

My son lived a "grow up fast" first five years with his mother. Family members surrounded him—his aunts, uncles, cousins, and family friends. At the age of five, he could cook, navigate his way around town as an adult would, and he had seen things that most grown men have not seen.

On July 3, 1983, I received a call from Muddear telling me that my son's mother had been killed. According to the family, EC Chandler hit her with a tire iron and killed her. He then took her to their home, cleaned her dead body, and placed a white sheet over her. EC sat at the kitchen table, smoked a cigarette, and called Muddear. I do not know what was said on that phone call, but I do know Muddear and Wes went out to the house. After entering the residence, Wes called the police. EC's arrest was swift, as murder charges were in his very near future at the jailhouse. The coroner came for the body, and word spread around Inverness like a California wildfire.

I received a call informing me that the mother of my child met the worst ending possible—murder. I immediately left Fayetteville, North Carolina, and headed for the Mississippi Delta. I drove that Torino all night, arriving in Inverness around three or four o'clock on July 4, 1983. Muddear told me where to find my son; he was with his aunt, Tynoon. I met Tynoon, and she handed him to me. We left for Muddear's house so we could talk more about what was happening.

I asked Muddear to keep WJ until I set up the house in Fayetteville to receive him, and she agreed. For the next six months, my son would stay at our home getting to know my side of the family.

I decided not to take him to his mother's funeral. For one, he was too young to understand. Two, I did not want him exposed to the drama following the tragic murder of his mother.

In six months, on December 23, 1983, I returned to Inverness ready to take my son back to

Fayetteville to live with me. I had bought a house and a reasonable car, and I had set up the house in a way that any child would love. We arrived back in Fayetteville on Christmas morning. When we walked into the house, he stared at the tree and all the toys around it. They were his. Walking down the hall to his room, there was his furniture, bed, television, and a closet full of clothing and shoes. I wanted to give him a stable living environment to grow up in, and I think I did just that.

Next to Sammy Smith, Joe Casey was the best friend a man could have. I met Joe in Dillon, South Carolina through a military friend named Hardy Miles. Joe was sympathetic to my son's situation, so he decided to move from Dillon to Fayetteville to help me raise my son. Joe became like a father to my son, and he was there to make things right for him. He took him to school, shopping, and just about everywhere he could.

I had to tell the Army that my son was with me, so I had a mountain of paperwork to sign indicating my son had care if I had to deploy on orders. Later, I found out that the paperwork already submitted was not enough. The Army, in my opinion, was harassing me about being a single parent. Despite the unofficial call to duty at a moment's notice and working later than usual regularly, my paperwork was in order. The "Army," or rather my redneck chain of command, was trying to pressure me.

Parents Teaching Children

To explain why man has not always made the best of things in life, I must attempt to investigate man in his beginning years. Babies are born dependent on their mom and dad, from which they inherit knowledge. The ability for the baby to learn could be genetic or it could use some work to develop.

Children learn many social, moral, and ethical beliefs from their parents. For instance, Baptist parents would likely raise their children with the same beliefs. This tendency is not limited to religion, it applies to almost all beliefs and values held by a parent.

I make this point because parents can only teach what they know how to teach. Culture and the stratification level have a tremendous impact on the development of a child. Parents always strive to give their children a better life or way than they had before them. How can we teach our children to be better than we were when we are teaching them to set goals based on our beliefs and values? Who is to say that these will apply when the child reaches adulthood? Even though we give them all the knowledge we can, it may not be as valuable to them as it was to us. The same rules we live by can be much different when they reach adulthood.

For a child to grow up well, they need to start learning at conception. Parents should not focus on issues that satisfy their immediate needs. Instead, they should focus on becoming healthier—mentally, physically, and socially—to support their coming child.

In our society today, women or couples who become pregnant are reluctant to do the right thing. They find it hard to change their immediate behavior. Work is usually the most pressing issue. Women will sometimes continue to work up until the time of delivery. Now how could this be healthy for a fetus? Almost all jobs or work is to some point stressful. The daily routine of rising in the morning and putting on our best image to face society can cause mental disorders to the fetus. Surely fatigue has an effect.

But do we, as human beings, realize when it is time to change? In my opinion, the answer is no. Humans have an inherited tendency to put things off. We do this because of our rearing. How many times were you told as a child that you could not have that toy and wait until Christmas for Santa Clause? Or wait until the next payday when I have enough money. Just how much is enough money or better yet, how long should we put things off? These delaying tactics become rooted in our so-called operating personality. Characterized by our reluctance to face immediate personality needs.

Unknowingly, we relay these same tactics to our children. This behavior has a profound effect on a child's growing brain. The child may apply this behavior to his schoolwork, thinking he can do the work later or not at all. This is a hard habit to break, speaking from experience. I find myself repeating these same scenarios in my life.

There is no short-term solution to changing the way we groom our children to be successful in life. Counseling can only help those who want to change. Many people know the difference between right or wrong. We often know how to correct this behavior, but we don't. We are so accustomed to doing what pleases us that we ignore the consequences, assuming that we will deal with it when we are better prepared. There is no ultimate state of preparedness, but because we put things off, we do not change.

When the baby is coming and we still have not made the changes to our lifestyle, we promise ourselves that tomorrow we will do it. But we never take advantage of that tomorrow. The baby comes and we are not prepared. Since we are not prepared, we feel unbalanced. We still have not developed the skills needed to train and raise our offspring.

What happens next? We start to teach our children our bad habits. Usually, we inherited these habits from our own parents. We have begun to repeat our lives in our children's eyes. Raising them to be just like us because we have not accepted that there is a better way to live.

Growing up in the south can place a set of clearly defined norms on a child. Imagine going into a department store with a food stand in the 1970s, and your child asks if they can have a sandwich. How can a parent explain to their child that, because of his skin complexion, he cannot buy a sandwich from that counter? Tremendous responsibility and candor have to be used to explain this ordeal. What effects, if any, do you think this would have on the child?

I never did gain a clear understanding of this from my mother, but I soon figured it out. For many years, I had to force myself to accept the ways of society in Mississippi. I acted as if I did not need to stray across racial lines to mingle in society, and so did all of my surroundings. I accepted things the way they were until I realized that I was only learning the things that my mother learned from her parents.

The Need for Therapy

Today I realized that I needed Gestalt therapy to overcome this dilemma in my life. For a person to feel the need for professional counseling, he must first feel a need to change a certain behavior in his life. Before consulting anyone, a man will exhaust all other possible solutions. I am sure that, before I ask for help with my life, I will try almost anything to solve my own problems.

Naturally, one does not want to air their dirty laundry to the world. What if the neighbors find out? Or even worse, what if my spouse finds out about my obsession with drugs or other women? When we do good as people in the eyes of others, we tend to think we don't need help with our behavior. Only when our habits consume us do we turn to Jesus or a counselor for help.

Man does well as long as things go his way, but he seeks help when the tide turns. This is a critical moment for him. He may feel he is a failure just because he needs advice or help. Once he admits that he needs help, it is as if someone else starts to carry the load.

To counsel is the art of exchanging opinions and advice. The counselor is the person giving advice or counsel. Each counselor will have completely different theories when it comes to evaluating an individual. There are as many approaches to counseling as there are counselors. A counselor approaches each session differently.

During a session, a counselor must be flexible in selecting an approach. The problem, the client, the physical surroundings, and the time available all factor into choosing the best method. Based on these findings, the counselor can use a direct or confrontational way of solving the problem. Again, all factors must be considered favorable for this approach. Another approach can be indirect, where the session focuses on the client, causing him to take responsibility for his actions. This type is usually more relaxing as it focuses on self-discovery. It usually helps clients with low self-esteem by making them more self-reliant.

A counselor has to be a good listener. Even when the counselor thinks that they understand the client, they must resist the urge to give hasty solutions. The initial explanation from the client may not be the underlying problem.

For example, if a client rants to a counselor about suicide, it could be the result of something much deeper than his personality. The root of the discussion could be the loss of a close family member. In this example, a counselor may urge the client to talk about the deceased. By having them talk about this person, the counselor may find that the client is not dealing with grief well. The counselor may easily provide the corrective behavior by reinforcing the deceased's wishes.

The counselor's role is to listen without identifying with the client. They must analyze the client's problem with empathy while also thinking about an effective strategy for rehabilitation. A client may be at ease if they can speak more freely about the problems leading to the crisis in his life. The counselor's ultimate goal is for the client to have the tools to solve problems for himself.

Counseling has been a part of my life for many years. Because of my problem-solving skills, people have come to me in search of counseling. I've helped to solve family crises, work issues, and general conflicts. My greatest attribute is staying calm in crises so that I may defuse a situation. What many may not know is that I am just as excited about the situation as they are, but I choose to control my reaction. Several situations occurred in my life that evolved my personality in this manner. First, and most important, is when I learned that you can catch more bees with honey than with salt. In this saying, honey refers to kindness and salt refers to rudeness.

Most people who know me were once reluctant to communicate with me. They later confessed that I am an introverted person, so they assumed that I wouldn't want to talk with them. I tend to not meet people well. Only after observing a person's character will do I make myself open for communication. I think I am this way because of the mistrust I have in man. I don't feel that most people are genuine and that the initial intent of a new acquaintance is to gain something from you. Therefore, my guards are always up when it comes to meeting people.

Many times, I have placed my trust in man and have not measured up to being upright and trustworthy. Friends may come to you in a crisis needing money or even your car and expect you to help them. just because they have a so-called emergency, they expect you to act in their favor. If you don't, they may not consider you a friend anymore. You can even be Black-balled. I've learned to only give things that I can afford to lose because, oftentimes, favors are not returned. Whether it be financially, mentally, or spiritually, favors can cause discomfort.

In closing, we as human beings need help. Everyone should see a counselor at one time or another, some more so than others. There are situations that one person can deal with and others cannot. We do not know how our lives will turn out to be as we grow, but one thing is for sure: death. Many fail to plan for this occasion because we learn to put things off. Death being our ultimate end, we would rather someone else tend to the matter. For a family to do anything beyond having life insurance is rare. To me, when we are born, our death should be an issue to the people who bore us.

The Rise in Drug and Alcohol Abuse

Drug and alcohol abuse has hit our youngsters like a storm. It is one of the most perplexing and challenging problems facing us today. This problem exacts tremendous societal costs. Millions of tax dollars go towards understanding and combating this problem. In some cases, illegal drug use can start as early as age eight. It is in the school, on the playground, and in the home. Drugs and alcohol can be found everywhere—on school campuses, on street corners, and in the medicine cabinet.

With the development of the internet, anyone can order drugs and alcohol in the mail. The booming drug paraphernalia business has made the drug trade even harder to control. Rolling papers, cocaine spoons, and roach clips are available to kids over the counter. Only recently has the government placed restrictions on what youngsters can buy. Teens have an instinct to destroy some piece of society during a drinking or drug episode.

Drinking is an increasingly popular rite of passage for college students. Binge drinking is the consumption of five or more drinks in one sitting. It has been a growing concern at school campuses for several years. One in three college students abuse alcohol. The number of women who deliberately binge drink rose from ten percent in 1997 to thirty-five percent in 1994.

Many sociologists attribute alcohol and drug use to the rising availability. According to the 1977 book Rites of Passage written by the American historian Joseph Kett, destitute youths were viewed as troublesome, rash, and without a future. This created an environment for the separation of our youth from adults.

American Psychologist G. Stanley Hall published a two-volume work called Adolescence. He describes adolescence as a distinct stage in life that begins at puberty and invites inner turmoil. This view was used to justify the establishment of adult-sponsored institutions which separated youth from casual contact with adults. Youths went into the institutions beginning at middle school, then high school, and then on to college. They were then expected to develop life skills that most people learn from interacting with adults. Consequently, this concept of educating our youth has led to great misconceptions.

Many times, kids go into the world with little knowledge of themselves, and they don't know how to say no to drugs or alcohol. This leaves them vulnerable to others. Discussing alcohol and drug use to young people doesn't prevent them from wanting to fit in. When they enter a new environment and some seasoned abuser invites them to join a party, naturally, they will accept. Case and point: Scott Krueger was a first-year student at the Massachusetts Institute of Technology when he drank himself into a coma and died, leaving his parents in search of answers.

High schools and colleges across the country debate about what they can do to help students avoid tragic ends. It could always start as a night of fun, but without knowledge of self, anyone could end up like Scott Krueger. In local and college newspapers, businesses run on average three to eleven ads that promote alcohol use. Pete Brown, a faculty member at North Dakota State University, says that 80 to 85 percent of the students at his school indulge in alcohol use at some level.

There is no simple answer to why youths go through this crisis. Explanations range from neglect in the home, substance availability, a desire for social acceptance, and being emotionally imbalanced. Some youth view drugs as a way to escape the social pressures of growing up. Most would agree that the basic reason for young people's drug use rides on peer pressure, curiosity, and availability. Youths want to fit in among their peers. As parents, we must educate our children in the home by any means necessary.

Expectations Forced onto Men

Society expects a lot from a man. He must be cool under pressure, strong when he is weak, and happy when he is sad. The demand is upon him to be the primary pillar in the family structure with the ability to analyze and solve problems. His set expectation is to have the wisdom of Solomon when it comes to supporting his family. He is, based on custom, expected to provide a sufficient income for his family to prosper. The burden of shelter falls to him as well.

Evolution has changed this perception of man to a point where he is nothing more than a human being. There is one problem with that concept is: man has not realized that the role once bestowed upon him is no longer the way of life. When a boy turns eighteen many states consider him an adult, but many more consider the age of twenty-one as the legal age for an adult. In any case, man must be in control of his social skills and survive on his own.

Through his early years, a man must learn the ways of the world and develop the tools needed to be successful. Sometimes this conceptual image of man works, and he becomes successful and well-rounded. But, many times, men must go out into the world unprepared for the many obstacles that will meet them. Social, economic, and emotional attributes go unseen while a man is in the learning years.

Society assumes that man will ask questions if he needs guidance. I have often heard that the only dumb question is the one you do not ask. This statement, in a man's mind, may have a double-edged sword. To me, this statement merely means that even though your question may be dumb, you still deserve an answer.

Man has the hardest row to hoe. Society expects him to do well, and he strives to do just that. I often wonder why more men are running corporations than women. I also wonder why there are more men on Skid Row than women. Women, in my opinion, have a better understanding of life than men. They tend to be less ambitious than men are when it comes to gaining approval.

A man needs approval. He wants people to view him as a strong and intelligent leader of something. This is the way society portrays a man, and it is the reason we need to be re-educated in our role in life. We need to learn to be better husbands, better communicators, and better fathers. Most of us feel ashamed to cry in front of our spouses because we weren't taught how to deal with our emotions.

Using the Word "Nigga"

We use the word "nigga" with pride as if it is a status of distinction, but really, this could not be further from the truth. The word nigga, is the worst depiction of the BAR (Black African Race), as I define and see it.

When said by a white person, it becomes even worse. Even today, white men think they can emulate Blacks just by using the word nigga. Most of the time, when the white man uses the word, he is on some kind of drug. He usually ends up getting his ass whooped by the very people he is trying to be like. It is not a word to use in general conversation by any means.

HOW WHITE PRIVILEGE CHANGED US

Mr. Otis, the town's cop, was a fat, short, sloppy, and slouchy white man who hated Black men and loved the Black women. He walked with a slow swagger as if to insinuate the pistol hanging low on his right hip. It was 38 Special with a six-inch barrel. His arms were out on each side to present a bigger presence when he approached a Black man. Mr. Otis acted like he was ready to draw that .38 special all the time.

This white man walked into Black people's houses and acted as if he lived there; he'd go looking in the pots on the stove, perhaps getting a taste! Any sane person would ask, what the fuck? Is this man trying to show dominance and control over my house or is he an idiot? The answer to both questions is yes, not only is this white man presenting this appearance, he believes he is in control.

I saw Mr. Otis one Saturday evening sitting in his car across from town in Inverness. I was on my way uptown to get an ice cream cone from the drug store. The drug store was down at the end of the street, not too much of a walk. It only cost a nickel for a scoop and a cone. Once I got my cone, the rest of the world was gone. I walked down the sidewalk, licking the side of the cone that melted the most. It was just the right texture and the right taste for me; I was enjoying it. Nothing attracted my attention away from the taste of that ice cream and cone.

Then, I saw Mr. Otis with his pimpin' walk across the street and kick it into motion. A Black man was standing outside Mr. Kemp's store with his foot and back on the red brick wall. Mr. Otis walked to the front of the Black man, pointed his finger in the direction of his face, and was shaking it at him. He then reached down to his side, removed his gun from the holster, and pointed it at the Black man's face.

The Black man did not move a twitch, fearing the white man, Mr. Otis, might just shoot him like a dog in the street. Mr. Otis put the gun back in the holster, grabbed the Black man by the collar, and once again, slammed him against the red brick wall. He again pointed his finger in his face, drew the gun, and said some slick shit to the Black man.

Imagine a nine-year-old Black kid watching this blatant racism against a Black man. The moment was frozen in time; minutes had passed by without a blink, ice cream ran down my hand to the wrist running to the elbow, and dripping to the sidewalk. What was I thinking at that moment? I was thinking about a murder at a very young age. This traumatic event psychologically damaged me for life. Even though I was too little to kick his fat ass, my mind had done a lot to assess this asshole of a man who had no honor. The story I just told you is meant to condition you for what is about to come.

We went to church every Sunday learning how your blessings are always "Just around the corner." Thinking back, I wonder what religion we practiced before the white man force-fed my people his form of Christianity? I am sure my ancestors were not Baptist, Methodist, or Protestant, and so on, so what religion did my ancestors practice?

We also learned how not to piss off the white man; to always say "yassar" and to always call the little white boys "sar" (sir) too, even if you are twice his age. You learn to yield and wait your turn at every public place. You learn to go to the back door of the dentist's office if you want any kind of service. In Mississippi, you learn to not drink out of public water fountains even though the laws had forced the white man to remove the "colored & whites only" signs suspended over them.

Emmett Till

The most important cultural behavior learned during the 1950s through the '70s is never to look a white woman in the eye. This action could easily come off mistakenly as attempted rape or disrespecting a white woman. Older Black men know to look at the ground when speaking to a white man or a white woman. One other thing, if approaching a white person on the sidewalk, Blacks had to get off the sidewalk until they passed them by. These were the rules of the Jim Crow South. Unfortunately, a Chicago boy would prove too youthful in understanding the real dangers of the deep South.

Mississippi was a racist place and full of bigots; Blacks were being killed all over the state and no one went to jail behind it. Emmett Till was picked up overnight from his family's home for allegedly sassing or whistling at a white woman. His kidnappers seized him in the witching hours of the night and drove to Drew, Mississippi. In a deserted barn, they beat, tortured, and shot young Emmett. On August 28, 1955, the pre-teen Emmett Till's lifeless, tortured body was pulled from the Tallahatchie River. All of this violent hatred over a white woman allegedly claiming young Emmitt whistled at her. Many years later, the white woman confessed that her allegations were not true. The whole country bore witness to the murderous ways of Mississippi, as over 50,000 people attended his funeral. Emmett Till's mother insisted on having an open-casket funeral. Mamie Till never received justice for Emmett's murder.

The 1960s brought out the worst in Mississippi's white residents; Jim Crow Laws were used for anything—from looking at a white woman to being outside the house after dark. Jim Crow law, in US History, is any laws that enforced racial segregation in the South between the end of Reconstruction in 1877 and the beginning of the Civil Rights Movement in the 1950s. Jim Crow was the name of a minstrel routine (actually called Jump Jim Crow) performance beginning in 1828 by its author, Thomas Dartmouth Rice, and by many imitators, including actor Joseph Jefferson. The term came to be a derogatory epithet for African Americans and a designation for their segregated life5.

On a personal note, my family protected me from the brunt of the Jim Crow Era. I heard of it often but experienced it rarely if not ever, I knew there was no place for me to be in the white man's sight. The only time I remember coming close to danger is when Mr. Otis shot a dog in the street while we were outside playing and the time he slapped a Black man and pulled his gun. I thank my family for having such a high hedge of protection around us—not allowing us to go through what most of the Black Mississippi had to endure. I also thank God for giving my family prestige.

Medgar

On June 12, 1964, a shooter's bullet ripped through Medgar Evers. The shot came from a cowardly Klansman hiding in the bushes waiting to ambush the war hero. Medgar was returning home from an N.A.A.C.P. meeting. Hours before his assassination, President Kennedy delivered a television address calling for equal rights for all Americans and all races. Even though the President is asking for equality, the Klansmen still wanted to kill and dominate Blacks in Mississippi!

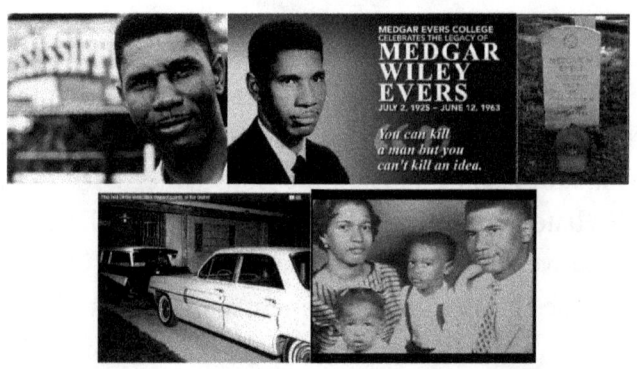

---

5 *Melvin I. Urofsky. Aug 20, 2018.*

Jackson, Mississippi is not far away from Inverness, where I grew up. For as long as I can remember, we have had relatives living in the Jackson suburbs. Each year when I am back in Inverness, my family never misses a time to visit the relatives in Jackson. They are Babe Ruth aka Velma Robinson, a longtime resident of Jackson, my nephew, Kevin, a transplant to Jackson from Inverness, and a slew of others I do not know. Jackson was the place to go if you want city living. Kevin was a barber who in my opinion is one of the best at what he does.

On June 21, 1964, James Earl Chaney, from Meridian, Mississippi fell victim to a racist assassination plot with his body buried in an earthen dam in the Mississippi country. Chaney was one of three civil rights workers murdered during Freedom Summer near Philadelphia, Mississippi. Mr. Chaney is another fatal victim of hatred displayed by whites for Blacks in America. The KKK killed the white men for associating with Mr. Chaney.

There was no reason for those three kids to be locked up in jail until nightfall to be released into the darkness. It makes me believe the white man hunted Black men as a sport. Once they were locked up, the sheriff called on his boys to round up and set up for the hunt. When they were in place, the sheriff released the prisoners to be hunted and killed. They would never admit it, nor will they ever take responsibility for it.

Sometimes I think they, white men, are the most ruthless, selfish, egotistical, and narcissistic species on the planet. They have fought with every other race on the planet and tried to rule over every other race on the planet.

A few years ago, no one knew that Cable News Network's (CNN) Don Lemon would be the most outspoken and militant Black man in television news today. Continuing his trend of calling it as he sees it, Lemon declared that white men are the biggest terror threats in the United States of America with travel bans against[6]

America seems to think that the world is blind to the treatment of Blacks. Some white males are terrorists and everyone knows it—including the FBI. Many get away with crimes from white-collar to any collar; keeping money, land, businesses from Wall Street to the money-hungry halls of Congress. Not all white men are bad, in fact, I have had discussions with them proving they understand our struggle.

So how do we change the ownership? We get registered to vote and vote, we take risks to win, we say what we feel and most importantly, we pool our money by supporting Black businesses. We as Blacks consistently spend in their stores, we consistently eat in their restaurants, we consistently want to live in their neighborhoods, stop it! We as Black people consistently give them our money, stop it! We as Black people must develop a better plan to execute and a better trust for each other.

National Matters

Born Malcolm Little in Omaha, Nebraska, in 1925, Malcolm X was the son of James Earl Little, a Baptist preacher who advocated the Black Nationalist ideals of Marcus Garvey. Threats from the Ku Klux Klan forced the family to move to Lansing, Michigan, where his father continued to preach his controversial sermons despite continuing threats.

---

[6] https://www.snopes.com/fact-check/don-lemon-terror-threat/

Minister Malcolm X, an African American nationalist, and religious leader was a Muslim and a human rights activist for the Nation of Islam. Malcolm X was an advocate for the rights of Black people; he condemned white America for crimes against Black America. White people remember him for the statement he made when John F. Kennedy's assassination took place in November 1963.

Malcolm X was talking about an old expression; "chickens out to pasture always come home to roost." It means, "What goes around comes around." He was referring to John Kennedy's assassination as part of the violence America inflicted on Black America and the world in places like Vietnam, Cambodia, and Cuba. This comment is famous because the Nation of Islam had censured him; Malcolm X was not to comment on the assassination of John Kennedy, on direct orders from Elijah Muhammad. He defied the order and was immediately suspended from the nation.

Malcolm X's suspension from the Nation of Islam lasted for ninety days, but his belief that the NOI was trying to permanently silence him caused Malcolm X to leave the organization for good. In New York City, on February 21, 1965, Malcolm's assassination by the government infiltrated rival Black Muslims tragically cut his life short. Malcolm was addressing his beloved new Organization of Afro-American Unity at the Audubon Ballroom in Washington Heights. Mr. X is included because he is an admired and inspiring pioneer of confidence in Blacks in America.

Hold your head high, do not turn the other cheek, and arm yourself to fight back against anything questioning a Black Man's manhood! Malcolm X was a real Black Prince! He was the strongest Black man at the time standing up and saying what he believed to be true. He did not bite his tongue or stutter with his words when he spoke. The white man feared him, and he knew it. They feared him so much that the white man paid the Black man to participate in orchestrating the assassination of Malcolm X. The FBI's J. Edgar Hoover wrote many notes about getting rid of the problem Black man, Malcolm X. Since his death, I know of no one to take up the baton and get down to educating the Black man and woman about how to survive in white America.

First, a Black man has to love himself and be thankful for what his ancestors went through for him to be on the stage. The Black man also has to realize he needs therapy; no way we can assume that the trauma our ancestors suffered did not pass on down to us. We are a damaged group collectively and need help. We also need to be thankful to our ancestors for suffering the most for us.

Black History in a Positive Light

Bass Reeves is the legendary and original "LONE RANGER," here is another story of how the white man stole the character of a Black man and made TV shows and movies of it. Mr. Bass Reeves was born in 1838, living until 1910. The real Lone Ranger was a Deputy US Marshal born a slave in the Arkansas Territory. He grew up in Lamar and Grayson Counties, Texas, where he belonged to Colonel George R. Reeves, who later became the speaker of the house in the Texas legislature. Mr. Reeves escaped going north into Indian Territory, becoming acquainted with the Cherokee, Creek, and Seminole Indians. He served as a soldier with the Union Army Indian Home Guard Regiments during the Civil War.

After the war, Reeves settled as a plantation owner in Van Buren, Arkansas. On occasion, he served as a guide for deputy marshals because he knew the Indian Territory very well. Reeves had once boasted that he knew Indian Territory and I quote, "like a cook knows her kitchen." As a result of his skills and knowledge of the territory, he was able to make substantial money as a tracker scout. In 1875, Judge Isaac Parker commissioned Bass Reeves as a Deputy United States Marshall. He is believed to be the first Black American to receive a commission as a deputy US Marshall west of the Mississippi River.

Deputy Reeves worked for thirty-two years as a deputy marshal in the Indian Territory. He was the only deputy, to begin with, Judge Parker and work until Oklahoma became a state in 1907. Mr. Reeves, stood six feet, two inches tall, weighing 180 pounds, and became a celebrity during his lifetime in the Territory. Mr. Reeves was an expert with his pistol and with his rifle. Newspapers stated that he killed fourteen outlaws and arrested over three thousand fugitives during his career as a peace officer. Deputy Bass Reeves, known as the "Lone Ranger" would frequently ride with an Indian while tracking in the Oklahoma and Arkansas territories. This is another story about our past where a white man was given the honor that the Black man earned.

Deputy Sheriff Bass Reeves
"The Lone Ranger"
1938 – 1910

On December 5, 2010, Deputy US Marshal Bass Reeves was officially inducted into the Oklahoma Law Enforcement Hall of Fame. US Marshal John Lloyd attended the ceremony and accepted a medal commemorating Bass Reeves' induction on that historic day.

In November 2011, the state legislature of Oklahoma passed an act officially declaring the bridge that crosses the Arkansas River between Muskogee and Fort Gibson, Oklahoma as the "Bass Reeves Memorial Bridge." Federal, state, and local officials along with Bass Reeves's descendants attended a dedication ceremony to officially name the bridge in Reeves's honor. Oklahoma State Senator Kim David presented US Marshal John Lloyd a ceremonial replica of the bridge sign to be displayed in the offices of the Eastern District of Oklahoma.

Blacks experience stolen legacy far too often, the feeling of hopelessness is a daily battle to gain recognition, not only in the Mississippi Delta but also all over the United States. The white man barely allowed Blacks to be educated in the Delta; he only supported Blacks going through elementary school and then going to work in the fields on the plantation. When it comes to the way Blacks suffer racial mistreatment, the only difference between northern and southern Blacks is the weather. Blacks learned basic English, just enough to know how to sign a name and know-how the history of the white man unfolds as his boss.

There are so many reasons why the Mississippi Delta and the city of Inverness are important to Black People's history; one, the Emmett Till murder, two, the Medgar Evers Murder, three, the proximity of Roy Bryant to the home where I grew up. In 1956, after the Emmet Till Murder, Roy Bryant, Emmett's killer, went back to work in his store as usual with one big difference; Black people said hell no to spending money there. Roy Bryant took a job in Inverness, less than one hundred feet from where I grew up, I was not born then but still, the very thought is chilling. The legacy of discrimination and low pay for Black Delta workers shows the power of racism over Black Mississippians even after the murderous rage of whites and the constant clouds of death hanging over many lives after the 1950s and 1960s.

In 1956, he went to the Bell Machine Shop in Inverness, Mississippi, and learned welding with the help of the GI Bill. Remember during that time, the government denied Black Veteran access to the GI Bill. Blacks could not use the Bill to attain any level of schooling. The government told the Black Veterans to go back to being a gravedigger, plumbers, or carpenters. Here we go again, this man was convicted of murdering Emmet Till, he was so in the loop for "white privilege" he got the job at Bell Manufacturer and had the federal government pay for his training to do so.

Not only did the federal government discriminate against Blacks coming home from World War II, but other elements of the federal government also did the same thing. I never knew Roy Bryant worked there until I became a man and had enlisted in the military. My oldest brother Theodore worked at Bell for nearly twenty years. Many of the Black men in Inverness worked there on and off for many years. I probably would have taken even more stuff from that place as a kid if I had known they catered to the Ku

Klux Klan. Bell Manufacture left tons of materials lying outside with no way to protect it from being stolen, so if I needed a piece of steel, all I had to do was take it.

The white man made us hate them; you may ask the question, how do I come up with a hate theory? Well, imagine the Black man as a hard drive for any computer and now look at who programs the computer. The white man programmed the computer to operate a certain way but eventually, a virus creeps in. The virus causes the data input to corrupt itself so the data no longer follows its programming correctly. So, what do you do? You bring in more data (Willie Lynch Speech of 1712) to force the data to operate the way you want it to operate. The data works for a while until the virus starts to figure out the routine. Once Willie Lynch's input merges in the system, the virus starts to take over again and you have a Nat Turner experiment.

Nat Turner (October 2, 1800 – November 11, 1831) was an enslaved African-American mystical preacher who led a two-day rebellion of enslaved Black people in Southampton County, Virginia, beginning August 21, 1831. The rebellion caused the death of approximately sixty white men, women, and children. The virus may not get very far, but the damage done is significant and the virus accomplished its purpose to corrupt the system of the white man's data input. So how can we be the blame for operating the way the white man programmed us?

They, the white man, took our ancestors from Africa, cleaned the hard drive, and reloaded it with the white man's information thereby creating the Black American Race (BAR). We are the BAR and we function differently than any other race on the planet. The BAR is a sole entity operating in America with our tools installed on our hard drive. How can you blame what you created for being what you created? The movie Frankenstein is a clear depiction of what the white man tried to create in the BAR. Frankenstein was, in the beginning, a very calm created person. He then becomes hard to control, understandably so.

The Emancipation Proclamation of 1865

On January 1, 1863, in a retreat home about three miles from the Union Capital, President Abraham Lincoln wrote and issued a proclamation historically named the Emancipation Proclamation.

The Emancipation Proclamation stated, "All persons held as slaves within the rebellious states...henceforward shall be free."

The Emancipation Proclamation, on paper, freed the slaves in the Union States and had little effect on the bordering Confederate states. This order did not actually free any slaves at the time; however, it did help keep Great Britain and other European countries from recognizing the Confederacy.

It also gave Blacks the right to join the Union Army. Nearing the end of the Civil War, nearly 200,000 Blacks joined the Union Army and Navy. In Texas, the Confederate government refused to acknowledge the Proclamation. On June 19, 1865, approximately ten weeks after General Robert E. Lee surrendered, Union General Gordon Granger arrived in Galveston to deliver the proclamation freeing the enslaved in Texas. Today, we celebrate July 4 as America's Independence Day, but the real day for Texas receiving the official notification that the slaves are free, is June 19, 1865. "Juneteenth," the 19th of June is celebrated as Black American's official Independence Day in Texas and around the US.

What I want to say about the Emancipation Proclamation of 1865 is that imagine at one point two million slaves becoming free as a result of the Emancipation Proclamation of 1863. Slaves walk off the plantation looking like tens of thousands of cattle grazing across the range, not knowing where to go, or a single thing about survival in the white man's world. All pretty excited because they are now considered free at the government level. Many slave plantation owners said no, but hell no to the end of slavery!

The Emancipation Proclamation of 1863 reminds me of the fishponds of the Mississippi Delta; catfish are grown in ponds specifically designed for this purpose, they feed on a schedule and get harvested in bulk. The process is barbaric and the result of greed; Black men get in the pond at one end, all the way across, they walk on a line with a fishnet driving the fish to one end. Once the fish are corralled at the end of the pond, a machine sucks them up into an aquarium on the back of a large truck. They are then transported to a processing plant, offloaded onto a conveyor belt tail first.

The next thing the fish knows, it's missing both fillets and is free falling into a big container to die. Even before the fish dies, the container full of carcasses is off to the boiler to get cooked, and then dehydrated. Nutrients are then added to make it healthy for the fish. This is what they now call catfish food. The white man feeds the recycled carcasses to the fish in the ponds and the cycle repeats itself.

Unfortunately, the newly freed Blacks have no money, they have nowhere else to stay, and they have nothing in the world to help them survive off the plantation. What do you do? Turn your ass around and go back to the plantation. That has to be the worst feeling a man can have. You see, the plan to free the slaves was not a complete thought concerning the slaves. The main concern was a threat to the south over the Civil War. Everyone heard about the forty acres and a mule that was never delivered. Even the ones that did receive the forty acres and a mule would have it repossessed by repatriated rich planters thanks to President Andrew Johnson. Socially, slavery was supported by law and the groups of white supremacists all over the south.

Abraham Lincoln issued a preliminary Emancipation Proclamation on September 22nd, 1862. It stipulated that the South had to a cease-fire or the slaves would be freed. The South did not take the threat seriously so they kept fighting, so on January 1st,

1863 the Proclamation went into effect. Mind you that not all Southern States were included in the Proclamation. Meaning that President Lincoln did not give a shit about the slaves, his concern was always with preserving the Union and appeasing the border states.

That is right, not all southern states freed the slaves. For instance, Kentucky had the Union Army all over the state and so did the Port of New Orleans. Even though the big deal is "Lincoln Freed the Slaves," it is technically a damn lie. Never forget, this move was to cripple the south by releasing 65,000 slaves. The sad part is the freed slaves by law could not be called citizens, they were to be called Freedmen. Thus, the surname Freeman, a derivative of the word Freedman was commonplace among Black cultures in the United States of America.

My grandmother was Nancy Freeman – Robinson, born in 1893 somewhere around Inverness. We called her Aunt Nane. Aunt Nane had a big house in the back of Inverness. Her home was one of the originals just outside the town's dump; the rest of the homes in that area were built after they covered the dump and sold the land by lots to Black people.

My favorite people were Nancy and Lealla, they were special needs persons and my friends. Today they still live together in a nursing home somewhere in Mississippi. Ida Bell, Willie Mae, Jorene, and Clyde all were very close family to me. Clyde is the last one living in Inverness, Ida Bell passed away, Willie Mae and Jorene moved to Greenville.

The "Freemen" Black was not considered a full man, or a whole man. Even though they were "Freedmen," they were still not respected as citizens. In context, the Three-Fifths Compromise in Article I, Section 2 of the Emancipation Proclamation allocated Congressional representation based on the whole Number of free Persons and three-fifths of a person for Blacks. Under the Fugitive Slave Act Clause, Article IV, Section 2, "No person held to service or labor in one state would be freed by escaping." In other words, the escaped slave is considered a fugitive and if caught, would be returned to the plantation. Although time passed and "freedom broke," as many formerly enslaved described the moment freedom was at hand, white citizens did not respect their citizenship unless the Union Army was enforcing the 13th, 14th, and 15th Amendments with force over the southerners.

Dred Scott

The Fifth Amendment—which states that "No person shall ... be deprived of life, liberty, or property, without due process of law." In the case of *Dred Scott v. Sandford* argued 1856 - decided 1857, the Supreme Court ruled that Americans of African descent, whether free or slave, were not American citizens and could not sue in federal court. The Court also ruled that Congress lacked the power to ban slavery in the US territories. Yet another blow struck against the enslaveds' futures and the immediate lives of the few free Blacks who never experienced slavery—the Dred Scott decision was damming. I mention this case because even with the Reconstruction Amendments, Black freedom in the minds of white southerners remained moot points in their reality—and their violence and vitriol showed as much.

United States Black Troops

Lincoln declared in the Proclamation that Blacks of "suitable condition, could serve in the armed service of the United States." Five months after the Proclamation took effect; the War Department of the United States issued General Orders No. 143, establishing the "United States Colored Troops." By the end of the war, over 200,000 African-Americans served in the Union Army and Navy.

With the Emancipation Proclamation enacted, the aim of the Civil War changed to include freeing the slaves. Although the Proclamation initially freed the slaves in the rebellious states, by the end of the war, the Proclamation had influenced citizens to accept abolition for all slaves in both the North and South. The 13th Amendment, which abolished slavery in the United States, passed on December 6, 1865. Although we are now freed Black men, we still have shackles metaphorical and real—on our feet.

Plessy v. Ferguson

In **Plessy v. Ferguson** (1896), the Supreme Court considered the constitutionality of a Louisiana law passed in 1890 "providing for separate railway carriages for the white and Black races." The law, which required that all passenger railways provide separate cars for Blacks and whites, stipulated that the cars be equal in facilities, banned whites from sitting in Black cars and Blacks in white cars (with exception to "nurses attending children of the other race"), and penalized passengers or railway employees for violating its terms.

Homer Plessy, the plaintiff in the case, was seven-eighths white and one-eighth Black and had the appearance of a white man. On

June 7, 1892, he purchased a first-class ticket for a trip between New Orleans and Covington, La., and took possession of a vacant seat in a white-only car. Duly arrested and imprisoned, Plessy was brought to trial in a New Orleans court and convicted of violating the 1890 law. He then filed a petition against the judge in that trial, Hon. John H. Ferguson, at the Louisiana Supreme Court, arguing that the segregation law violated the Equal Protection Clause of the Fourteenth Amendment, which forbids states from denying "to any person within their jurisdiction the equal protection of the laws," as well as the Thirteenth Amendment, which banned slavery.

Because of the Emancipation Proclamation, and more so the 13th Amendment, Blacks were free but in extreme danger of being killed by hanging, burning, castration, capture, and returned to slavery by another name in the peonage system. Blacks left the plantation with nothing; four hundred years after the white man gained a foothold in America. Here is an example of how whites exuded power and discredited Blacks by using tactics of creating strife and confusion. How desperate can a race of people be? To continue the use of crookedness to control and to want the power over a people. Ladies and gentlemen, I present to some and introduce to others, "The Willie Lynch Speech of 1712."

The 1712 Speech by Willie Lynch

In 1712, a slave owner from the West Indies named Willie Lynch gave a speech to the colony of Virginia. The Virginia slave owners requested Willie Lynch because they were having problems controlling the slaves at the time. Mr. Lynch had devised a plan that guaranteed to control slaves and it was working in the West Indies. His speech follows in its entirety.

"Gentlemen, I greet you here on the bank of the James River in the year of our Lord, one thousand seven hundred and twelve. First, I shall thank you, The Gentlemen of the Colony of Virginia, for bringing me here. I am here to help you solve some of your problems with your slaves. Your invitation reached me

on my modest plantation in the West Indies, where I have experimented with some of the newest and still the oldest methods of control of slaves.

Ancient Rome would envy us if my program is implemented. As our boats sailed south on the James River, named for our illustrious King whose version of the Bible we cherish, I saw enough to know that your problem is not unique. While Rome used cords of wood as crosses for standing human bodies along its old highways in great numbers, you are here using the tree and the rope on occasion. I caught a whiff of a dead slave hanging from a tree a couple of miles back. You are not only losing valuable stock by hangings, but you are also having uprisings, slaves are running away, your crops are sometimes left in the fields too long for maximum profit, you suffer occasional fires, your animals are killed, gentlemen, you know what your problems are: I do not need to elaborate. I am not here to enumerate your problems. I am here to introduce you to a method of solving them. In my bag here, I have a foolproof method for controlling your Black slaves. I guarantee every one of you that if installed correctly, it will control the slaves for at least 300 years. My method is simple, any member of your family or any overseer can use it. I have outlined several differences among the slaves and I take these differences and make them bigger. I use fear, distrust, and envy for control purposes. These methods have worked on my modest plantation in the West Indies and they will work throughout the south. Take this simple list of differences, and think about them. On top of my list is "Age," but it is there only because it starts with an "A," the second is "Color" or shade, there is intelligence, size, sex, size of the plantation, status on the plantation, attitude of the owner, whether the slaves live in the valley, on the hill, east, west, north, south, have fine or coarse hair, or is tall or short. Now that you have a list of differences. I shall give you an outline of action-but before that, I shall assure you that distrust is stronger than trust, and envy is stronger than adulation, respect, or admiration. The Black slave, after receiving this indoctrination, shall carry on and will become self-refueling and self-generating for hundreds of years, maybe thousands.

Don't forget, you must pitch the old Black versus the young Black and the young Black male against the old Black male. You must use the dark skin slaves versus the light skin slaves and the light skin slaves versus the dark skin slaves. You must use the female versus the male and the male versus the female. You must also have your white servants and overseers distrust all Blacks, but it is necessary that your slaves trust and depend on us. They must love, respect, and trust only us. Gentlemen, these kits are your keys to control, use them. Have your wives and children use them, never miss an opportunity. My plan is guaranteed, and the good thing about this is that if used intensely for one year, the slaves themselves will remain perpetually distrustful. Thank you, gentlemen."

With this speech being relevant to the times, I do acknowledge that some Black historians regard this speech as a hoax, but it remains important in my eyes and the context of our history. Between the sixteenth and eighteenth centuries, European nations began to colonize the Americas enslaving approximately 12 million Native Blacks Africans. Let that sink in for a minute, 12 million enslaved Native Blacks and Africans. The slaves were brought for the labor aspect alone, to work the plantations and mind the silver and gold mines. Tribes such as the Hausas, the Mandingoes, and the Krus had built societies that strived for spirituality and commerce. The English, the Dutch and the French had established trade with these Tribesmen making the merchant ships a welcome sight to see anchored off the coastline of Africa. They imported guns, cloth, and other products manufactured in home countries to trade with tribal chiefs in exchange for slaves.

The Slave Trade initiated separatism in the Americas, creating segregation by race, as a permanent cultural attribute in our American society more than anywhere else in the world. Not only did the English, Dutch, and French prosper from the slave trade, many African tribes gained riches by trading people for guns and clothing. Traded slaves often came from warring tribes and the local prisons. When these populations were low, the chiefs made available the people of his tribe. These individuals were often of and from low strata families. Once an African was captured, they were chained together two by two, right leg to the left leg. Even though they were all Africans, language and tribal background were very different. Slaves were taken from thousands of villages and towns throughout a 3,000-mile stretch of the African coastline.

Captives sometimes had to travel as much as one hundred miles to the coastline where they would be imprisoned at Fida until the Europeans arrived. Fida was the name of a prison encampment located near the coastline. Hundreds of buildings and slave castles built along the shore provided housing for the slaves. The captives were frightened and confused about the imprisonment. Many had never broken laws or imagined being captured and/or imprisoned. When the ships arrived the slave traders stripped them naked and examined men, women, and children from head to toe by a so-called ship doctor. If they were found fit and in good condition, they were set aside for the voyage to the Americas. If found to be over the age of thirty-five, with defective limbs, eyes, or teeth, they were rejected and given the name of **Mackrons**.

Mackrons were considered not marketable for the auction. Those who passed the examination would receive a brand on the breast as cattle do. This mark would signify French, England, or Dutch ownership. They were then rowed out to the mother ships for passage to the respective countries. Nearly three hundred slaves were packed in the hull of ships for the voyage across the ocean. Slaves were kept underneath the ship's deck fifteen to twenty hours a day when the weather was good, and more than twenty-four hours during inclement weather. Each slave occupied a space five to six feet long, sixteen inches broad, and two or three feet high. Slaves often had to lay in vomit and defecation for long periods. The stench in the hull of the ship was intolerable and dangerously infectious.

The heat from the ocean climate, the closeness of each slave caused many deaths before the ship reached the Americas. Women, men, and children helplessly waiting for the break where the slaves would be taken above deck to stretch and breathe fresh air. Many slaves, out of frustration and dismay, jumped overboard during this opportunity rather than suffer the fate awaiting them.

Virginia had acquired thousands of slaves to plantation its tobacco plantations. With the slave population steadily increasing, Virginia had trouble controlling the slaves they owned. Virginians were seriously frightened by slave uprisings. From 1663 to 1859, the colonies would still experience a series of slave rebellions. Nat Turner led a religious rebellion in Virginia sending the slavery system into turmoil. He rallied about seventy slaves and went on a rampage from plantation to plantation killing 55 white men, women, and children. They burned and destroyed the property of slave owners and enlisted the slaves along the way. The rampage was over when Nat Turner and his followers were no longer able to secure more ammunition. At this point, they disbanded and eighteen of them were eventually captured and hanged for the conspiracy. This is just one of the many rebellions against slavery in the colonies, Gabriel Prosser, Denmark Vesey, and Nat Turner were all revolutionary leaders of men fighting to be free from the bondage of slavery.

Willie Lynch set an extreme level of demise for the Black man and so did segregation. His letter made every turn as rough as a gravel road, his letter made every man and woman of color doubt the validity of having a healthy relationship. In 2018, the remnants of Willie Lynch still exist among Black people. We do not trust each other nor do we support each other in Black endeavors. Yes Sir, the Willie Lynch letter of 1712 made the impact it intended for Black people. After combating Willie Lynch at every turn in life, I was delighted to read the presidential address of the one and only Nelson Mandela. Nelson Rolihlahla Mandela was a South African anti-apartheid revolutionary, political leader, peace activist, and philanthropist who served as President of South Africa from 1994 to 1999. He was the country's first Black head of state and the first elected in a fully representative democratic election. Here is his speech in its entirety:

Our deepest fear is not that we are inadequate
Our deepest fear is that we are powerful beyond measure
It is our light, not our darkness, that most frighten us
We ask ourselves
Who am I to be brilliant, gorgeous, talented, and fabulous?
Actually, who are we not to be?
You are a child of God
Your playing small doesn't serve the world
There is nothing enlightened about shrinking so that
Other people won't feel insecure around you
We are born to make manifest the glory of God that is within us
It is not just in some of us; it is in everyone
And as we let our own light shine, we unconsciously
Give other people permission to do the same
As we are liberated from our own fear
Our presence automatically liberates others.

If only white America would embrace the truth of its democracy, would Black America fully thrive? These historical notes have a recurring theme I will continue to explore and illustrate.

Desegregation?

May 17, 1964 – the Supreme Court announces that segregation of public schooling was illegal. The announcement meant that the first step to desegregate belonged to our children. Black children had to attend school with white kids. Sounds simple enough, doesn't it?

Desegregation has a lot of requirements set in motion; the biggest and most destructive of the Black community was bussing. During segregation, Blacks attended school among people who looked like them. This simple factor made it easy to learn. If you look at all the famous and inventive Blacks, they all went to school with people who looked like them. There they flourished in life and creativity.

The purpose of desegregation was to give Blacks the same materials as the white kids received. Yes, Blacks received better facilities, better books, and better classrooms but psychologically, the mentality of the Black child suffered. As a result of desegregation, Blacks were carried out of their neighborhood and into a place where they were hated? They had to fight to get through the front door; remember the Little Rock Nine? Nine kids had to fight to attend the white school. It took the National Guard to escort them into the school.

I went to an all-Black elementary school and an all-Black high school. In the Mississippi Delta, there is still segregation in the school system. There is a white high school and a Black high school. In the newspaper, each year there was a separate homecoming, a separate prom, and an all-white football, baseball, and track team. I graduated from Gentry High School in 1977, it is a very popular school in the Mississippi Delta, and I am proud to have been a graduate of an all-Black school. No matter where the bus took us, Black people were still Black no matter where we went to school or how desegregation and bussing may have moved us. Kids were subjected to the brutality of racism and bigotry seen before and during the Civil Rights Movement.

Racism and The Vietnam War

I watched my oldest brother forced to serve in the United States Army. Tho did not want to go. After reluctantly honoring his "draft papers," he enlisted as an ammo handler destined for Vietnam. We loaded ourselves in the car and left for the Greenville bus station, it was time for my brother to get on the bus journeying to the Jackson Military Entrance Processing Station (MEPS).

My mother and I went on to downtown Greenville for her to do some shopping at Stein Mart. We eventually headed back to Inverness. Driving past the Chinese-owned stores in Inverness, we saw Tho standing on the corner. He beat us back to Inverness. The Army had to come and get him, which they did, about three weeks later.

Tho received his training and shipped out to Vietnam where he joined up with a Black group called the Dee Mau Mau. Vietnam, according to Tho, was as segregated as Inverness so it was nothing new to him. The Dee Mau Mau was a militant Black organization looking out for the welfare of Blacks in Vietnam. I tried to research the organization but could not find out much about them.

As an infantryman and an ammo handler, Tho's placement meant being on patrol a lot during the year he was deployed to Vietnam. Each time he led the patrol into the bush, they all returned to base. Tho developed a streak of luck leading patrols into the bush. One morning as they geared up to hit the bush, the sergeant told Tho to get on point, Tho reminded him that he had been on point several times during that week. The sergeant did not care; he wanted my brother on point.

It was then when my brother made a choice that haunted him until he died. He leaned his weapon against a tree and sat down on a stump. Shamefully, the white Army in 1968 did everything they could to stress the Blacks in Vietnam. That day, the entire squad was killed while on that same patrol. In my opinion, Tho had a vision that day and the vision saved his life.

His story about serving in Vietnam drove me to do research on the country and find out more about the war. The following paragraphs are about Vietnam and I dedicate the curiosity to my brother, Theodore Ricks who served in the United States Army as an Ammunition Specialist during the Vietnam War.

Vietnam extends some twelve hundred miles south of China's frontier to the Gulf of Thailand covering an area about the size of California. Vietnam is more than 127,000 square miles of beautiful diverse land, 1,500 miles of coastline, and approximately 900 miles of bordering land. Mountains and valleys contrast with miles of rice patties, lush green fields, and flat treeless grasslands. There are small pockets of deserts in Vietnam, but about half of the country is covered with jungle, and nearly four-fifths of the land has tropical vegetation.

Vietnam, then (1940-70) had a population ranging around 35-40 million people, the area's population density averages sixteen hundred to about two thousand people per square mile, which is a density almost twice that of Rhode Island, the most densely populated area in the United States. Vietnam is divided into three distinct geographical areas; Tonkin in the north, Annam in the center, and Cochin-China in the south.

Vietnam's growth as a nation is largely similar to that of the United States. When the original thirteen colonies became overpopulated, and jobs became harder to find, Americans migrated out West. The Vietnamese migrated from their ancient homeland of China's southern provinces. First, they took Tonkin, then Annam, and not until the nineteenth century, after centuries of warfare, settlements, and colonization, did the Vietnamese fulfill their destiny by winning Cochin Chin from Cambodia.

Tonkin, Vietnam's northern rice basket, is a large fertile plain of about seventy-five hundred square miles. Vietnamese founded this as their first settlement. Tonkin's soil enrichment comes from many waterways, primarily by the Red River, which is sometimes referred to as the "Mother River." Flowing southward from its source in China's Yunnan Providence, the Red River deposits rich, fertile soil throughout the Tonkin's delta. The Red River connects to the Haiphong, via the Thai Binh River.

During the Vietnam War, Haiphong served as the North's primary port for receiving Russians and Chinese military aid. Initially, the United States urged the bombing of the Gulf of Tonkin to no avail. It was not until May 1972 that President Richard Nixon ordered the mining and bombing of Haiphong, virtually. Halting the flow of military aid through the harbor during the rainy season, the Red River would rise to dangerous levels, sometimes rising more than thirty feet above the low lands through which it flows.

Floods occurred several times a year with little warning. To make the land in Tonkin manageable for living, the Vietnamese devised intricate systems of dams, canals, and dikes enabling them to manage the flow, and overflow of the Red River into the Tonkin Delta. Over the years, many immense systems of dams, canals, and dikes constructed improved the infrastructure. The dikes protecting Hanoi were so vital that during the 1960s and 1970s the North Vietnamese hired peasants in emergency labor battalions to maintain and strengthen them against airstrikes from the United States.

Networks of canals also link the Tonkin's Delta Rivers. The canals provide water for irrigation and were used to transfer water from one rice patty to another. South of Tonkin and the Red River Delta is Annam.

The mountain people, better known as the "Montag nards" traditionally inhabited a strip of land, which in some places is only thirty miles wide. More than thirty-three tribes of Montag nards existed in the Annamese highlands. Because of their isolation, the presence of Malaria, and few developed agricultural resources, the Montag nards are still sparsely settled and populated.

Although sparsely populated, the highlands were strategically important during the Vietnam War. In 1954 HO Chi Minh solicited the help of the Montag nards living along the Annamese highlands, successfully recruiting more than ten thousand tribesmen north of Hanoi. There they were trained as teachers, medical technicians, and political Agents. Ho Chi Minh also established self-governing zones for the Montag nards and gave them substantial representation in the National Assembly in Hanoi.

The South Vietnamese had little success recruiting the help of the Montag nards. They still referred to them as "Moi" or "Savage." Saigon attempted to assimilate the Montag nards by force. In turn, they met resentment from the Tribesmen. Later, the South Vietnamese government would further alienate the Montag nards by relocating catholic refugees into land traditionally held by them.

In 1960, the United States entered the scene, with an attempt to rebuild alliances with certain strategically located tribes of the Montag nards. The Central Intelligence agency and Army intelligence agents had some success enlisting support from the Rhade Tribes. General William Westmoreland would later praise the inspiring courage of the Hre tribe which held off an entire enemy regiment at Camp Kannach, a United States Special Forces outpost in Binh Dinh Province.

Despite the efforts by the United States, long-festering racial animosity between South Vietnam and the Montagnards prevented cooperation. In 1966, President KY and the South Vietnamese government reluctantly agreed to respect the Montagnard tribal and property rights. To show that this agreement was in good faith, President KY appointed a tribesman as Special Commissioner for Montagnards Affairs. South Vietnamese military officials promptly violated this agreement.

Further north in the Annamese highlands, the virtually unpopulated Khe Sanh was the site of one of the most important battles of the war. For seven days the United States Forces resisted an all-out North Vietnamese attack. The North Vietnamese attack on Khe Sanh brought to mind the communist defeat of the French forces at Dien Bien Phu in 1954. Combined United States and South Vietnamese Forces finally broke the attack at Khe Sanh, shattering two of North Vietnamese best divisions.

Annam, with its many rivers and long coastlines, provided both food and transportation for its occupants. The many natural bays along the Annamese coast compensated for the obstacles of overland transportation made prevalent by the mountains.

More people lived closer to the South China Sea which supplied an abundance of salt and fresh fish. Maritime pursuits have always been important to the Vietnamese coastal dwellers, however, just as South Vietnamese neglected the importance of the Annamese Mountain Tribes, they also neglected the importance of the high seas. Montagnards, the original dwellers of the Red River Delta, proved to be a valuable asset to the North and South Vietnamese fighting Forces but were never employed to their full potential as soldiers.

They were skilled coastal sailors and expert navigators in the highlands. A French soldier told journalist Lucien Boda: I have the Sedange as allies; they are great big good-looking fellows with nothing on except paint and tattooing and magic charms. They are red like copper.... They fight against the neighboring tribe, the Katai, who is on the side of the Viets, and just as we do with the Sedangs, the Viets Officer stake on the Katai and train them.

Cochin China is the southernmost frontier of Vietnam. Winding for more than twenty–five hundred miles, the Mekong River runs from the Tibetan highlands and empties into the South China Sea. Until the nineteenth century, much of Cochin-China was virgin territory and richer than the intensely cultivated regions in the north. More subtle than the Red River, the Mekong rises slowly in the rainy season, reaching its height around October. Plantation owners were able to plan their labors without fear of flooding as in the north. Since the Mekong River floods rarely, inhabitants of the south did not need to replicate the dams, dikes, and canals as in the north.

Much of Cochin-China furrows by streams and canals that create an excellent network for navigation and irrigation. Barges maintained communication between the smaller villages and carried the farmer's rice to Saigon, Vietnam's biggest port located some forty miles from the coastline. Under French rule, Saigon became the capital of Vietnam and later grew into a metropolis area with billions of dollars of United States aid. West of Saigon lies Cambodia, which also became part of Vietnam's war theater of operation. Many United State Soldiers remember areas like the Parrots Break in Cambodia. More than two thousand North Vietnamese troops died here and nearly eight thousand bunkers succumbed to US bombardment at the Parrots Break.

Vietnam is located in a tropical zone; in the far south, its latitude line aligns with Panama. No other factor, human or natural, affects the rhythm of life as the monsoon season. Vietnamese plan every aspect of life around the monsoon. Between May and October, the monsoon blows from the southwest of the Indian Ocean bringing tremendous typhoons, heavy rains, and summer heat. Vietnam's average rainfall is about fifty-nine inches per year, slightly more than that of Miami. An average of seventy-two inches of rain falls on Hanoi alone.

Monsoon rains became a way of life for the American Soldiers. The rain and dampness seeped into the skin, rotted clothing, and turned boots sickly orange in color. Some United States troops did not wear underwear during this season because underwear caused jock infection. American soldiers normally carried forty pounds of gear, which made movement virtually impossible during the monsoon season. The French and the United States forces knew that they could not compete with the monsoon rain as the North Vietnamese Forces. At the battle of Dien Bien Phu, the French became mired in mud after a steady pounding rain had soldiers stuck in three feet of mud.

Malaria, leeches, and many ailments besmirched the United States ranks causing severe non-combat casualties through the monsoon season. In the war against Communist insurgencies, the US forces could not fight at potential and performed very poorly. Tanks and artillery became useless in seas of mud rendering sophisticated equipment helpless against the North Vietnamese forces. Air support was at a near standstill, thirty-minute missions would take hours during the monsoon.

In 1973, the American Military entered into a cease-fire dictated by the Paris Agreement. Under the Presidency of Richard M. Nixon, United States Soldiers began to pull out of Vietnam. President Nixon pledged to continue financial aid to South Vietnam. America had not succeeded in its attempt to deter communist aggression in Vietnam. Fourteen North Vietnamese Divisions with one to two hundred thousand combat-ready soldiers would stage for the attack on Saigon, and on 27 April 1975, North Vietnam took over the capital of South Vietnam, rendering Vietnam a Communist country.

Back to Life on the Homefront

I left Inverness on my way to the United States Army on August 26, 1977. Life would never be the same from that point on. I finished boot camp and Active Individual Training (AIT) at Fort Knox, Kentucky, and on to Fort Bragg in 1978. Fort Bragg became my Segway to finding my manhood in life.

My first assignment was Alpha Company 25th Signal Battalion; it was an organization full of telecommunication people. Anytime another organization went out on a field training exercise, the cable dogs had to go with them to establish communication between the organizations. I was a young cat still a boy learning my way of serving my country as a light-wheeled vehicle and power generation mechanic. Mechanics were needed on the exercises as well so I would go out to the woods as support personnel. I contributed my ability to adapt to outdoor living and woods to being a boy scout with troop #349 in Inverness.

The troop taught me how to march, it taught me my left from the right, how to half step; make a right face, and how to salute. When I entered the military, I was right at home with discipline. I worked very hard to learn and be good at my job as a mechanic. Because of my hard work, I earned a promotion from E-1 through E-4 in about eighteen months. As a mechanic, I learned how to repair vehicles and equipment well. I repaired from the M151A2 Jeep to the Gamma Goat, CUCV, and onto the famous deuce and half truck. My deuce and a half truck was known as the bumper number, Alpha 68; it had an A-Frame mounted on the back used to hoist heavy equipment to the bed of the truck. Alpha 68, all geared up, turned out to be one of the best trucks in the battalion and I knew that because it was my truck.

Everything went well in the motor pool as long as I was a good worker, kept my mouth shut, and kept my ass in the motor pool fixing trucks. I watched the white mechanic, Kessler, get selected for schools without asking and get promoted a month or two before me every time. It took a conversation I had with the motor sergeant, Sergeant Boyd to get me moving in the right direction. Sergeant Boyd told me the way to get around all the bullshit was to volunteer for every class, every mission, and every assignment that came down the pipeline and I did.

Once I volunteered, I started to get exposure outside the motor pool meeting people and not spending all my time underneath a freaking truck! The surprise missions kept coming, the first sergeant would come out to formation and announce the upcoming training, and I was the first to sign up. Once there was a mission to get on an airplane; I took it and once we were on the plane and while seated, men with automatic weapons busted into the aisles and shouted in a foreign language. This was a long time before the hijacking of 9/11; it seemed like Special Forces doing a series of training on hijacking an airplane was a strange coincidence for the future.

Another training I volunteered for is the Recondo Training; I have nothing but respect for anyone who wears the Indian Arrow Badge. It takes an elite individual with un-touchable discipline to complete the fourteen-day training plan. Recondo was the toughest, most challenging course I have ever attended. We learned hand-to-hand combat in the sandpit, hasty repelling from towers, cliffs, and helicopters, navigation from nowhere to somewhere nearly twenty-five miles away. Yes, Recondo is a challenge for the toughest man.

All the training added up the points for greater promotions, I made it a point to keep up with my scores. I think because I was effective in managing my military career, the leadership took direct aim at me. Trouble for me began with everything done on behalf of my career.

My first Article 15 – While attending yet another school, I was learning to rebuild engines. I had a 302-ford engine with a two-valve carburetor. The last three weeks spent at Central Texas College working on rebuilding the engine would pay off. It was in the air, ready to slip it back into the 1973 Gran Torino. I rolled the a-frame to the car with the engine suspended in the air and then, the phone rang.

Alpha Company had put on a called alert. An alert, in the military means we are about to go to war so get your shit and report to the motor pool. I left the engine suspended thinking this was yet another fake alert. Once I arrived back at Alpha Company, everyone packed and stacked to go on a convoy, so this time it was real. Alpha Company ended up going on a field trip for the next forty-five days.

When Alpha Company returned thirty-five days later, everyone had to go into recovery. Cleaning equipment, cleaning weapons, vehicles and standing in long lines to get our M16A2s turned into the armory. I knew this was going to take a while, so I decided to lock my M16 in my wall locker and run over to Central Texas College to finish what I started, putting the engine back in the car.

After about three hours or so, I realized my M16 was in the wall locker so I rushed back over to the company. When I arrived, everyone was on stand-down looking for a weapon. It was my weapon they were searching for so I took it to the armory and turned it in. Then the first sergeant called a formation and dismissed the company. On Monday morning, I was being served.

Second Article 15 – Captain Smitz ordered me to put tires on his jeep, I replied, "Yes sir! I will put the tires on your jeep, have the driver bring the jeep to the shop."

Captain Smitz said to me, "I do not want to hear any of that bullshit from you, Sergeant Smith, just get some tires on my jeep."

Again, I repeated myself, albeit differently. The one thing I had on my side was the regulations, which states do not work on a vehicle unless the driver is present. The next day, no driver showed up with the vehicle so the captain did not get new tires on his jeep. Again, they were attempting to railroad me so I received my second Article 15.

Third Article 15 – As a buck Sergeant, I was in charge of dispatching vehicles for the duty driver. Keep in mind I had been given the worst of the worst vehicles and equipment naturally because I am a Black Buck Sergeant among all the white buck sergeants. My crew had been there in the motor pool for the last six months trying to get that old equipment operational and ready for battle if the time came upon us. The duty driver had slipped my mind and here it is six p.m. in the evening.

I told my mechanic, Specialist Denarola, to take these bolt cutters and bring up the first vehicle that would start and he did. Before the vehicle went out the gate, I took a roll of duct tape and taped the numbers on the bumper. I thought I could get away with it since it was the weekend. Then I remembered the vehicle was going to sit in front of battalion headquarters as the duty vehicle. Someone with a curious mind decided to pull the duct tape off the bumper, revealing my swindle.

Fourth Article 15 - While attempting to keep the company from blaming me because all the vehicles in Alpha Company were on the deadline report, the captain made the motor pool work seven days a week. Our team was making progress, but not very fast. One Saturday while up on a truck checking for an air compressor leak, the captain's driver showed up telling me he needed a dispatch. I lost it; I cursed that white boy too much, so much that he started crying.

I went back to working on that truck and just happened to look up, Sergeant Dawson had the cat in a bear hug. He had found a pipe and was heading back over to hit me with it. While Sergeant Dawson held him, I jumped down from the truck, walked over to that kid, and started cursing again.

The one line I remember saying to him is "Motherfucker, if you hit me with that pipe, I will have your ass out of the Army before the sun goes down!"

At that point, I was furious; I told Sergeant Dawson to tell First Sergeant Miller, I quit and if he needed me, he could find me at home. I left the motor pool and went home really thinking I had quit the United States Army. About an hour or two later, I received a call from First Sergeant Miller.

He said, "Now Sergeant Smith, you just cannot quit the Army," and I agreed.

I told him I let my anger get the best of me. He said to take the rest of the weekend off and he would talk to me on Monday morning.

It is hard not to tell the truth about how dirty the white soldiers were back in the early 1980s. I kept going to school and watching my points. To get a promotion to Staff Sergeant, one had to obtain a certain cut-off score. A cut-off score indicated how many points a soldier had to qualify his/her for promotion to the next higher rank. My score was at the eight hundred levels, which was enough points to get the promotion.

Somewhere around February 1983, I made the cutoff score in the Army Times newspaper. I assumed that the white captain and first sergeant would come down to the motor pool and congratulate me for a job well done. No, they did not; in fact, they said nothing to the contrary, but the tone was "get that row out boy!" I kept it moving knowing that I had made the cutoff score for promotion to staff sergeant.

Six months went by before I had a day to go and visit a place called "MILPO." Military Personnel Records is where they kept my 201 file. So, I go to this place and ask to review my records, and the first thing I see when I open the folder is a copy of promotion orders promoting me to staff sergeant. I am highly upset by now, my commander, Captain Smitz, and First Sergeant Smith deliberately avoided recognizing my promotion. The Army squared up with me by paying back pay and providing a public promotion.

I am now a staff sergeant, E-6 and at twenty-four years old, the youngest staff sergeant in the battalion. This was great on my part, but terrible for the white people. Seems to me, they, the white people devised a plan to get rid of me. Article 15's are tools used by the military under the Uniformed Code of Military Justice that is similar to a misdemeanor charge in the local governments. By this time, I had received four or five article 15's and was nearly at the end of my contract with the Army.

This is when I realized I had been in the Army for nearly five years and haven't accomplished a damn thing. I was afraid of going back to Mississippi and living my life out and accomplishing nothing significant. I knew I needed to re-enlist; the only way to do this was to not have all these Article 15's. I went to see the Battalion

Commander, who is in charge of everyone. I told him that I felt the chain of command targeted me as a Black and not as a soldier; this is why they have issued me as many articles as anyone in the battalion.

Colonel John T. Lawrence III immediately told me that he was issuing a set aside order and that he would speak to the commander of Alpha Company. When he did, Captain Smitz resigned as the company commander and I was able to reenlist for another six years. Fortunately for me, I changed from the motor pool or from a 63B30 to a 15E34. A 15E34 in the Army is known as a Persian Missile Crewmember and the number four is considered an instructor identifier.

I left Fort Bragg and traveled to Fort Sill, Oklahoma to attend school or reclassification. Here I trained to operate a Persian missile, a nuclear weapon. At the time, I possessed a top-secret security clearance; this allowed me to receive details about the nuclear weapons capability. Picture this; a Persian Missile is longer than a Wal-Mart tractor and trailer. It is so long that the nose has to fold alongside the stage two-proportion unit. The warhead is transported on a separate vehicle and is mated to the proportioning unit just before it is time to launch the missile.

My job was in the Platoon Control Center (PCC); when a fire order came, we inserted the key into the lockbox, removed the card, snapped it in half, removed the message, and started the decoding process. The sheet has one thousand numbers and letters. The code sheet had a sequence such as "column 43 and row 16," whatever letter is located at that position becomes the letter in the launch sequence.

Once fifteen or twenty numbers and letters have been coded, the numbers then become the grid ordinance for the target of the missile. This is where my calling to teach became evident; I received an instructor position at the Non-Commissioned Officer's (NCO) Primary Leadership Development Course (PLDC). This course taught junior NCOs how to become professional NCOs. I taught leadership, communication, map reading, compass, land navigation, first aid, and many more classes. I worked for Michael Warren, the Commandant of the Academy; he was a very knowledgeable boss and friend. As an instructor, I learned a lot about communication and teaching to those who may have learning disabilities.

I joined the Masonic Fraternity while living in Lawton, Oklahoma through Mistletoe Lodge # 31. There were nine of us on the cable tow going through the degree work. I was extremely fascinated with masonry; the craft taught me how to be a better man. I was with a group of younger men who were the first young group to go through degree work in the Oklahoma Jurisdiction. I heard that the older guys had to decide to bring in younger recruits because the older ones were dying off. Either way, masonry is a beautiful story veiled in allegory. I know it was there and, in my heart, I felt like I became a man.

DECISION TO JOIN THE MILITARY

Army Schooling

It takes a lot to finally look back on my life and admit I was a High School Failure. I smoked weed, drank beer, wine, liquor, and tried a little cocaine. I was so bad that I failed Mrs. Shortridge's English class during my senior year. That was my cue to enroll in summer school. If I had skipped summer school my whole trajectory would have changed; you see, I would not have joined the military. So, I went to summer school, earned my diploma, and left Inverness on August 26, 1977. The Greyhound bus traveled to the Jackson Military Enlisted Processing Station (MEPS). This was my first time traveling on a bus. I enjoyed the ride.

Once in Jackson, I experienced my first taste of military living. The yelling of orders like stand here, turn there, stop moving around, put your feet on the yellow footprints and shut up were the norm at the MEPS station. I went through medical taking shots in both arms along with everything checked physically. On to the job assignment, a 63C10, tank mechanic; this was a long six months in training. The job was later changed to 63B10, light wheeled vehicle mechanic and, of course, infantry. At Fort Knox, we went through taking shots, issued green uniforms, tops and bottoms. Socks, drawers, t-shirts, and boots as part of the issue; they gave us everything, even a toothbrush, and soap.

I had a white friend while in boot camp named Fred Self; Fred was from the Hollers of West Virginia. One thing I remember learning from Fred was how to cut a deck of cards with one hand. Fred had the look of a redneck but was a friend during boot camp. Fort Knox was a hard training base. There were four hills named Misery, Heartbreak, Agony, and Defeat. We climbed or ran the hills Monday through Friday for the eight-week boot camp. These hills were hard to climb every day, I will never forget them. If you took Basic training at Fort Knox, you will never forget them either.

After boot camp, the Mechanic school was next. I went to diesel mechanic school for six months; I learned how to pull the pack (engine), perform lube and services on diesel engines. As soon as I left Fort Knox heading to Fort Bragg, North Carolina, the army changed my military occupational specialty (MOS) to 63B10. Meaning I was a light-wheeled vehicle and power generation mechanic. and became very good at it. We serviced jeeps-M151A2, trucks-M880, deuce & a half, 2.5 ton, M35A2, and 5-ton trucks. I was so good at it, the engine sounds got embedded in my mind. I could listen and tell the driver what was wrong with his truck. I got assigned to Alpha Company's 25th signal company, which at the time was nicknamed the "Alpha Dogs." During those days, profanity and derogatory words were the norms. One thing I learned while assigned to the Alpha Dogs was to apply myself to every opportunity presented for education.

There was a time when the First Sergeant came out with a Reconnaissance School offer. A lieutenant and I were the only two to apply. This led me to get in the best physical condition of my life. I ran an eleven-minute forty-five-second two-mile, was able to do hundreds of push-ups and side straddle hops. Later, as I found out, this was a Recondo training experience. Recondo is a school for the elite foot soldier. The average soldier could not make it through the course, it's like training for the military Olympics. Recondo is a fourteen days pure hell training in the forest. Every day consists of mud, catching live chickens for food, building rope bridges to cross rivers. It also has "dropping" from a rope forty feet above the water, demolition, and more. After completing the Recondo course, I received the Indian Head Patch, a very rare patch issued by the 18th Airborne Corps.

I left Fort Bragg heading to Fort Sill, Oklahoma for yet another school. No longer was I a mechanic, I am now a 15E30, Persian Missile Crew Member. The Persian Missile was an intercontinental ballistic missile. Meaning this missile can hit the target in another country. It was as long as a tractor-trailer and shot out flames like the space shuttle rocket when launched. The Persian is a nuclear-capable weapon capable of destroying everything within a five-mile radius. Each time we rolled out to a launch site the German citizens protested. They threw themselves in the street blocking the way of the missile transport.

The name of the place was Schwabisch Gmund at a camp called Heart Kansern. My duty was to field artillery units. Most of the time people ask what is your MOS? The answer would be 63C10. When the Army decides to send a soldier from the leadership academy, primary leadership development course (PLDC) to recruiting school over drill sergeant school, it is an honor and a curse to attend the school of their choice. I applied to go to drill sergeant school at least six times and each time received a denial. After the sixth time, the Army sent out orders for me to attend recruiting school. At the time, I was a teacher at PLDC; the drill sergeant school was in the same complex so I watched them daily going through the motions. With the selection for recruiting duty, I was pretty much content with the Army's choice. As a recruiter selectee, I attended recruiting school in Indianapolis. At the military base, Fort Benjamin Harrison. The training was twelve weeks of paperwork, rehearsals, and learning how to be a salesman in the Army programs. The programs broke down into "TEAMS." The T for Training, E is for education, A is for Adventure, M stands for Money, and S is for Service to Country.

As a recruiter in Worcester, Massachusetts, I found the job of recruiting very hard to learn. Worcester is forty-five miles east of Boston and approximately ninety miles west of Springfield. It is the home of KAHR Arms and WPI, Worcester Polytech Institute. While attending the school, they brought in Lee Debois, a famous salesman from the nineteen nineties, to help us learn how to sell the Army. Selling an intangible product, selling a dream to way fair and high school boys, girls and dropouts started very hard to do. It has a lot to do with location and demographics. As you read earlier in this book, I am a native Mississippian from the poorest of regions in the United States. I asked the Army to assign me at or near a recruiting station in any southern state to match me somewhat in dialect, character, and knowledge of the area. These motherfuckers sent me to Worcester, Massachusetts, a city about forty-five miles exactly east of Boston.

It took me nearly six months to learn the recruiting program in a way to make it work for me. Once I got into the groove of getting them in the Army, it was easy. I made a gold badge in less than two years recruiting over ninety, seventeen, and eighteen-year-olds. My statistics were so good, I got voted the number two recruiter for the Boston Recruiting Battalion in 1989. The only person who did better than I was stationed at Fort Devens, MA. Recruiting duty requires a lot from a soldier. You are no longer with the Army; you are on your own in a strange city attempting to sell the Army. Sometimes, as a recruiter, you are lucky and end up recruiting at or near your home of records or where you grew up. You wear the uniform of your branch; for the Army, I wore the Dress Blue and Class B Uniforms nearly everywhere and the people loved it! Everyone wants to have an audience with a soldier, airmen, Marine, and sailor. My day started when most people's days ended. As people were getting off work and schools were turning out, I was gearing up to go to work on getting them signed up.

All the branches of services operate in the same office building out of separate offices on Main Street and downtown. The military service spending the most on advertisements usually gets the best office view of the street. Worcester is a typical northeastern town greatly populated by white people. The assignment was not difficult, just not where I wanted to be. The station commander was Martin Ascole, he was Italian and always seemed to act like he was always listening deeply to you. He seems to be fair and I never had any real issues with him. Sergeant Bobby Grinnon was the reserve recruiter, there were a few other recruiters in the Army's office on the grind, our goal was to make a mission and go fishing. Each day, Monday thru Friday, the station had "Red Time." Red Time is when each recruiter pulls up a high school database and goes down the list dialing number and making contact for appointments from the book of numbers. The government purchased names, addresses, and phone numbers of every kid who reached eleven and twelve grades. This occurs all over the country The goal was to land at least three appointments before red time was over.

Why did the federal government decide to send me to the northeast corner of the United States? I could never answer that question. While there, I got assigned to a vocational high school, a hands-on mechanically inclined high school with a work environment. I also had Doherty Memorial High School, a college prep school, and an all-girls high school. Worcester Vocational & Technical (Votech) High School was my best-recruiting ground. The principal and I had a great relationship; he allowed the Army to do the kind of recruiting that made me a star recruiter. The other services were there as well however, they were not as successful. Doherty High School was my second-best school but I did not like recruiting there. The students seem to view the military as a last result and not an option to decide upon before graduation. The principal was very nice to the recruiters so I never had issues getting into the school or having access to the students there either. I recruited at the local colleges and from the street; every person who was of age and could walk was a target. Both areas were fruitful, whereas they all wanted/ended up with the Infantry.

The infantry provides the recruit with loan repayment. Repaying money borrowed for school, and loan forgiveness with a five-year enlistment into Infantry. Living and working in Worcester was awkward; I drank liquor every day, nearly becoming an alcoholic, for real. I wore dress blues to the club, drove the hell out of the government car, and used every resource available to get people to join the Army. I was very successful as an army recruiter. Would I do it again? Hell no, I hated it! Naturally, I had to find the Black neighborhood and there was none. I found the Africans and the Puerto Ricans but no Black neighborhoods. An old man once said, when given lemons, makes lemon aid, so that is what I did with the Massachusetts assignment. I patrolled the schools, the malls, the streets, and the restaurants for potential recruits. While on recruiting duty in 1989, the government was in negotiations to end mid-range nuclear weapons in Europe. The name of the treaty is the Intermediate-Range Nuclear Forces Treaty, (INF Treaty).

Two Jobs, A Family, And a Twist

The signing of the INF Treaty did not affect ninety-five percent of the military but it did affect me. As discussed earlier, my job in the military before recruiting duty was 15E34, Persian Missile Crewmember. This job was a powerful one; I had the responsibility of handling a nuclear weapon. After completing military MOS training, they offered me a position at the Non-Commissioned Officer (NCO) Academy on Fort Sill. I would be the Primary Leadership Development Course (PLDC) Instructor. While there, I taught at least 400 young sergeants, male and female, how to become Non-Commissioned Officers. In one particular class, there was a young lady named Joyce attending my class. I saw her and immediately became attracted to her. From that point on, we fostered a relationship and became very close friends. During the relationship, we conceived a child. His name would become Jacqua. After spending nearly three years at Fort Sill, I asked the Army if I could attend Drill Sergeant School but they never did respond.

I ended up getting selected for a twelve-week recruiting school at Fort Benjamin Harrison, Indiana. The school was in the heart of Indianapolis; a part of town for Black people. That was the hardest, well next to the most stressful class I have ever attended. Courses we RECX, (a recorded sales pitching exercise to join the Army and red time) calling at least twenty people an hour trying to make an appointment. I completed the school so I asked them to send me to an Army recruiting station in the south. I ended up in Worcester, Massachusetts. A recruiter's duty starts when everyone else is heading home. School is out and Mon and Dad are at the dinner table. I hated it there starting in the basement of a four-decker home. I found a house after about three months. For the first six months, I could not get the hang of recruiting using intangible methods. Later on, I became the super recruiter making missions and going fishing! I finished up with recruiting duty after a gold badge award by taking the option to help shut down weapons in Germany. I drank liquor as if it was going out of style.

Since the signing of the INF treaty, I was offered a choice to remain on recruiting duty or return to the line with soldiers to help dismantle the Persian missiles since it was a mid-range nuclear weapon. The 1987 Intermediate-Range Nuclear Forces (INF) **Treaty** required the United States and the Soviet Union to eliminate all nuclear and conventional ground-launched missiles with ranges of 500 to 5,500 miles. The treaty marked the first time superpowers agreed to eliminate an entire category of nuclear weapons. The United States and the Soviet Union destroyed a total of 2,692 intermediate-range missiles by the deadline of June 1, 1991. I took going to Germany rather than spending an eternity as a recruiter in Massachusetts. The Army had me pack up my gear in Worcester and leave for Schwabisch Gmünd Germany. I walked away from two years of recruiting duty and the opportunity to become a permanent recruiter (00R). Maybe if the Army had sent me to a southern state, I would probably have retired as a recruiter.

I spent nearly six months in Germany working with the Persian Missile Crews packaging up the nuclear missiles. Of course, that meant the school (15E30) was no longer a valid option, so I had to take another direction. George Bush senior wanted to send me to the new war that had just started, Desert Storm, as a supply sergeant. When the war started, on the hill, which is the nickname for Gmund, every soldier was called into the gym and briefed about the Middle Eastern situation. After the briefing, there was a roll call of officers and enlisted personnel. Once the roll call was over, the soldiers not called were dismissed. If your name was called, you were to remain in the gym until further notice. I was scared but lucky, my name was not called. Come to find out, the first group had shipped out overnight to a forward base being readied for deployment to the Middle East. Day two of the muster formation in the gym; around five that evening, another meeting in the gym revealing yet another list of names. Now, I am getting worried and feeling blessed that I was not called out for the deployment during round two. I left the gym this time thinking my luck was running out—and I was right. On the third day, everyone was ready for the third round of names to be deployed. This time, I was not so lucky. They made it to the last sheet on the last day to call my name for deployment to the Middle East during Desert Storm. This time, I stayed back; they told me I was going to a tank battalion as a supply sergeant in Bremerhaven, Germany. Fortunately, I had arranged through a friend who worked with assignments a day or two before they called my name. Just as they were telling me to pack up, I received a call telling me I was not going to the desert, but Fort Lewis, Washington.

The power of friendship is amazing, the plane landed at the Seattle Airport at 12:01 a. m. on January 1, 1991. We boarded a bus from the airport to Fort Lewis, Washington. Once there, it was time to relax and get used to being back in the United States of America.

I was assigned to the 295th Quartermaster Battalion, as a platoon sergeant. My military rank was an E-6, Staff Sergeant however, I was considered an E-6P, meaning I was on the list for E-7, Sergeant First Class. As usual, the first sergeant and I did not get along so well, one day he told me I could stay out at the Central Issue Facility (CIF), which was fine for me. I still made it up to the company for physical training (PT) in the morning; each run was anywhere from three to five miles and I loved it. There was Lieutenant Leakey, who was there to be trained by me and there was this old hunchback white man named Mr. Bender who used to piss me off all the time just to show he had a little power. Anyways, the job required me to supervise the issue and receipt of Common Table Allowance (CTA 50). CTA50 is every type of gear used by soldiers from pistol belts to extreme cold-weather gear.

Most of the time, soldiers turned in and received gear making the CIF the first and last place they visit when at Fort Lewis.

I will never forget what the guy I replaced said, "Do you see those crows sitting on top of the garbage can?"

I replied, "Yes, I saw them."

He said, "The crows are just like a bunch of Niggars digging through a trash can."

Those were his departing comments. It was nearing time to leave Fort Lewis, Washington, I received a letter from the Defense Reutilization and Marketing Service (DRMS). The letter made an offer for me to become a demilitarization Specialist with training in Battle Creek, Michigan. Of course, I accepted and was immediately sent for training in Battle Creek for the next four weeks. While there, I visited the Kellogg's factory, the Elks Club, and the DRMS training facility. After completing the course, I was sent to Nuremberg, Germany with duty at the Defense Reutilization and Marketing Office (DRMO). The flight to Germany was a breeze; it took every bit of eighteen hours to fly over the Atlantic Ocean. The first person I met at my duty station was Mr. Lonnie T, the Property Management Branch Chief. He became my first supervisor and trained me how to function as the Demilitarization Specialist. I never thought the government was so wasteful until I made it to this assignment; they threw away laptops by the dozen and then by the truckload. We had to crush them in the beginning. Later, someone realized the hard drives contained sensitive information and precious metals that should be removed before disposal. The government threw away jeeps, Aries K cars, washing machines, dryers, desks, tables, chairs, and so much stuff I could not keep track of. It was my job to handle everything coming in but more especially the stuff that posed a threat to the United States Government such as weapons, ammunition brass, and tank track. The government wanted to ensure these particular items did not fall into any foreign government's hands.

I spent three years in Nuremberg with the last three months in Kaposvar, Hungary. I had the opportunity to travel extensively while on this assignment. I went to Austria, France, Italy, and a few other places I care not to mention. One place that stands out in memory is Dachau, Germany, a concentration camp. Walking on those grounds, I could feel the souls of the people who died in that camp. How I ended up there is a different story, we were on vacation in Munich for the Oktoberfest drinking the liter beers and I was toasted. I ended up at the train station and boarded the wrong train that took us to Dachau. Decided to make the best of the trip so we took the tour and probably made history as the first Black group to visit the camp. I ended up going there with a couple of friends who were as lost as I was. To see the camps first hand is mind-boggling, the place is holy ground. Thousands of Jews lost their lives there. The furnaces and gas showers were still there; the furnace was similar to a giant wood-burning stove, big enough to fit a coffin, there were three of them. The gas chamber looked like a shower you find in a gym; the Germans told them they were getting a shower so their victims just walked in the shower. Once the chamber was full, the Germans would lock the door and turn on the gas. The atrocities of this place are unimaginably inhumane.

A New War Zone, Promotion, And Putting Congress to Work

The last four months in Europe were action-packed, many things were happening concerning the Bosnian Conflict. In February 1996, I was handpicked to travel into Bosnia and set up a forward DRMO for the soldiers deployed in the region. In getting there, I used a Jeep Cherokee vehicle turned into the DRMO as a leftover from Desert Storm. New Jeeps were donated by Japan in place of soldiers as their contribution to Desert Storm. My chain of command informed me that I would be in the region for less than ninety days. That was fine for me. I need to be back in Nuremberg no later than June 14, 1996. My son and daughter were to graduate from the Nuremberg high school on sixteenth June 1996; I had no choice but to be at my kids' graduation. The chain of command and I agreed to have me back in Germany in time for graduation. So, it was set that I was to depart with a white guy named Kevin P. Sullivan. Sullivan and I were the same in rank, both Sergeant First Classes, (E-7) with one secret; I was an E-7 (P) promotable. Before I was assigned to the DRMO, I made the E-8 list, so it was a matter of time before I received my additional stripes.

We left Nuremberg sometime in February 1996 in route to Kaposvar, Hungary, which is on the border of Croatia. We drove through Austria and on into Hungary. Crossing each country's borders was very delicate but we did not have any problems getting there. The road trip was beautiful; how many Americans can say they drove from Germany to Hungary? Not very many. Once there, we lived in a makeshift barracks with World War two bunk beds and mattresses. Accommodations were poor at best, not a place to call home. A kiddy table in the room was used for meetings and eating. Every day, I left the security of the Army compound to go out and conduct assessments of property left in Bosnia. It was a lot of work to do and there was so much property abandoned by the American government.

The DRMO leased a building outside the military compound, they called it DRMO Alpha. Before long, we had trucks bring in items like washing machines for the soldiers to re-purpose. On any given day, I received tractor-trailers full of materials, many trucks were sent back to Germany to the Equipment Redistribution Facility (ERF). I finally received my number for promotion to Master Sergeant in the Army. Lieutenant Colonel James Childress had the honor of giving me a promotion ceremony in a combat zone. Little did I know this promotion, again, would bring out the racist behaviors of my white counterpart. I am now the senior noncommissioned officer assigned to the region for the DRMO. Within a week, they shipped the white boy out of the region back to Germany as if they did not want me to be in charge of him. No problem, we came there together, they promised a return at the same time so I assumed we would be leaving together. He left in the middle of the night claiming he had a family emergency. How wrong was I to believe these white folks were on the level with me; none of the chains of command wanted to give me an answer about departing back to Germany. I asked everyone all the way back to headquarters in Germany; no one responded to emails or phone calls. All I wanted to know was when I was going back to Germany.

Since I could not get an answer, I wrote a four-page letter, indicating all the calls and emails sent to command with no response. I decided to give them a few more days to respond and they did not. After feeling abandoned, I wrote a letter to Thad

Cochran, a Republican senator for the state of Mississippi. Within a week, he responded stating he would look into this matter and get me the answers I so desired. For those of you who do not know what that means; a Congressional Investigation is now underway for the command I am assigned. This is a major blow for the commander, Colonel Gustafson, he would never make general with a congressional investigation on his command record. Suits him well for not answering me after repeated requests. After the start of this investigation, none of the officers spoke to me about anything; they treated me like I had the plague. Within a week, I was told to pack up and go to the tarmac to board a C130 aircraft for the trip back to Germany. The plane broke down, so I went back to the barracks until the next day. The next day I sat on the tarmac until the next plane came in and that C130 was deadlined too. One the local chain of command got wind of the mechanical failures of the aircraft. The same jeep we used to get to Bosnia was used to transport me to the Budapest International Airport. Airman Roy drove me to the airport and the command paid for the flight back to Germany. Made it back there on June 15, 1996; I remember this well because graduation was on June 16, 1996. I enjoyed every moment of watching my kids graduate from high school the following day.

After I settled back in Nuremberg, I went back to my place of employment at the DRMO. I was treated as if I had the plague or the Black death or something. No one in my chain of command would speak to me. Each time when I went to speak with Matthew Platt, he was either too busy or not in the office. With forty-five days left in Germany, I did not have time to keep looking for someone to approve my departure back to the United States. Therefore, I took it upon myself to clear all places in Germany. I cleared all the records required to include getting airplane tickets for my family. Finished detaching myself from Germany. Finally cleared heading to the airport, boarded the plane for America, and on my way back to the real world.

Landing back in the United States, I made my way back to Inverness for a thirty-day leave. I had no idea that Little Rock was a go-between for my next assignment. They started by telling me I would be stationed in Little Rock, Arkansas for my last duty station with the United States Army. Deciding to splurge a bit, I made a sweet high-end purchase of a new BMW. After a few weeks of enjoying my brand-new ride, it was time to report to work. I was excited about living in Arkansas, it is close enough to go back to Inverness at a moment's notice yet far enough to stretch out and visit other places. I arrived at the 96th Reserve Support Command on a Monday, did some preliminary searching around to find out exactly where I would be. The administration official told me I would be further assigned to Ada, Oklahoma. I did not want to go to Ada, but I left the Command and that day and drove on to my assignment. Ada had a population of about 12,000 in 1996. I reported to the reserve center there in Ada, hung around several hours then drove around the city on my way out and back to Little Rock.

I felt like this was a setup for failure, the center in Ada was full of white people in military uniform, not looking like soldiers, but like militant white men in military uniform. I did not want to fight another fight against prejudice after leaving Bosnia a month ago. The military representative in Washington at the pentagon could only offer two choices, one in Salt Lake City, Utah, and the other in Ames, Iowa. Never would I have thought the Army would be so selective at the end of my career. I chose Salt Lake City; when it was time to go, Dwayne White took the trip with me in the brand new BMW 318i. I had not long ago picked it up in New Orleans, Louisiana at the Navy shipyard. The military ships a military man's vehicle any time he is deployed overseas. I sent one car over there and had one returned. The pickup location is usually at the soldier's discretion. We plotted the trip and rolled out of Inverness driving through to Utah. The city was nice and clean, I did a drive-by the office and headed on to see Ogden and Layton, Utah. Ogden and Hill Airforce Base were linked hand and hand. Looked at several places to live for the first few days with Layton beating out Ogden because of the location. Layton was conveniently located within Salt Lake City so I leased a house in Layton just outside of Hill Airforce Base.

The Army has this base out in the desert in Utah called Dugway Proving Grounds, aka, "Area 52." Most of us are familiar with Area 51, the place where all the aliens are kept but few people know about Area 52. My job was to train the reserve military organization on how to conduct logistical operations in multiple military theaters. Reservists came in on the weekend to conduct drills; each drill was a strategized layout of training of Regular Army military operations incorporated into the reservist way of life. Most of the players held full-time jobs as something else and could easily be viewed as out of place in a military uniform. During the week, I met with the Command Sergeant Major to develop the weekend schedule for incoming soldiers. It was an awesome assignment that left me unchallenged during the weekdays. I found myself going to the gym every day around noon to play basketball with the locals. Most time was spent reading and writing lesson plans for the reserve. Other times were spent training for and going out to participate in military funerals.

New Directions

My last assignment came when I visited San Antonio, Texas. The Utah organization had a mission at Fort Bliss in El Paso. When the mission was over, instead of going back to Utah, I went to San Antonio for three days. While there, I looked everywhere looking for a place to retire. The city has everything I'm interested in finding in a city. My guide took me to the north, south, east, and west looking at properties, school statistics, and prices. The northeast side of town in the suburb of San Antonio is a city called Schertz, pronounced like 'shirts,' had a new development going up and the lots were only $16.00 a square foot. It was the cheapest land sale in the city! I designed a 2,500 square foot house on one of the lots. I also had time to visit Fort Sam Houston, out of the several military bases here. When I saw an old friend, I asked for a position in his organization and got one. Back in Utah, I presented the change of assignment and received some pushback. The Mormons did not want me to go. The Utah duty assignment was in an old military facility overlooking Salt Lake and the University of Utah main campus. I had a beautiful corner office to leave behind and I was ready to go. Salt Lake City has no native Blacks; any Black there was imported. I lived near Hill Air Force Base next to the city of Ogdon, Utah. Ogdon has the largest concentration of Black people in Utah. Nowhere else can you find more than five native-born Blacks in any city in Utah.

Once they finished building my KB home, I checked out of Utah and into the San Antonio Army Medical Center (SAMC). Six months were left on a twenty-one-year career in the Army. I was assigned to the basement general supply unit. After checking in to let them know I am here, I spent the final six months of my military career at home working on a business plan.

Of course, I applied for jobs during that time, but no company wanted to pay a reasonable salary. Then, I met the Boeing Aerospace Support Center on Kelly Airforce Base. I was hired as a manager of logistics at a nice salary. There, we were to restore the Airforce KC-135 aircraft, also known as the Stratotanker, as close to new as possible. These guys were sloppy, going out drinking all night and trying to work on a plane does not mix! We had the KC-10 Troop and Cargo airplane and the C-17, one of the newest aircraft to the force. Working at Boeing was difficult at times, more so, for Army retirees. This made me stay on guard and put my armor on. Flyboys and Airforce retirees had even better jobs than I just because the color of their skin is white. Boeing is an undercover racist company. I lasted there six years before being laid off over a situation created by my peer manager.

When Boeing moved to San Antonio Boeing Aerospace Support Center hired me as a material manager in October 1998. I was in charge of the receiving dock with fourteen employees pulling the load. Accommodations, resources, and power were elements of working for Boeing. The job was very stressful at times. Especially when we could not find the items the mechanics needed to complete a job. The items were there at one time, but somehow during the move, they were lost. Word made it up the chain to management; who in turn sent Carlos, a Venezuelan and a Brigham Young University graduate. Carlos had a problem speaking English and he did not have a good grasp of the language. One day while in a meeting, I asked Carlos to codify a process he was attempting to make our section do. He had no idea what codify meant, so he lashed out with his authority.

He poked me in the chest with his finger and I said, "I feel threatened."

I went on to write about the incident about the finger in the chest. It resulted in Carlos being suspended for two weeks The layoff was a result of a peer manager, when Boeing won the contract for the KC-135s, they immediately needed warehouse space. The airplane hangar, Building 275, was not available until the first plane arrived. Hardware for the airplane came in by the tractor-trailer load. One of the old warehouse buildings in the near area became available for a temporary time. My peer, JD, functioned as a material manager for airplane hardware. His job was to receive the hardware and place the same material in a warehouse location. Locating the material in the warehouse was a process of checks and balances. Three things needed to happen; receive the material, find the proper location and enter that location into a database that will create an easy method of finding what is needed at the time of need. JD did a great job receiving the materials as they arrived from Sacramento.

Working in the warehouse was as usual until Boeing decided to bring the materials over to the main hanger. JD told management he could move and relocate the materials over the weekend. I repeatedly warned JD not to take on this assignment, we should outsource the move. Keep in mind, there are thousands of unique stock items to move and assign new locations. JD Began the process; I knew he had a plan to make this happen, right? The plan was to physically relocate the material with one or two guys he felt like he could trust. Twenty-four hours into the move, items started to back up on the receiving end at the hanger. Art was supposed to locate the material as fast as JD could move it to the hanger. For the first twenty-four hours, none of the material found its way to a hanger location. We later found that Art had not at all entered any of the parts moved to a location nor had he entered any of the items into the computer.

So, Monday morning rolls around, JD had been working all weekend and still had not reached the halfway point of the movie. Materials were laid out on the hangar floor without a location assigned to them. To find an item, we had to search through the items on the floor. Many times, the aircraft mechanics needed certain items and aircraft parts and we could not find them. Around Wednesday, he was still working on the move and just about to collapse from fatigue. He had failed the move, causing maintenance delays and schedules pushed back on the KC-135 Stratotanker. JD had no excuse available other than he just caused nearly a hundred people their jobs. He brought this on himself, attempting to please his bosses was sheer stupidity! About two months later, we were outsourced and laid off. Boeing hired an independent contractor to provide the necessary hardware. JD tried the impossible costing us our jobs and eventually his life, as he died not even six months later.

My section was told to go to a certain room where we would be given details of the outsourcing. In the room, we were handed an employment application. I refused to play along with the shenanigans. Later that same day, I was in my office thinking about what was happening and why, when two white guys from the new company came in. They wanted me to sign on with them. I said I would with a 10K raise and a two-year contract. They hesitated and then said that they needed to speak with their management and I said those are my terms. After about thirty minutes, I started packing out of my office to resign from my position with Boeing. Because I was part of management, I parked inside the gate and near my office making it easy to move out of the office.

With the mass movement of material and the outsourced department, surely, we were in for a surprise from Boeing. A layoff was unavoidable and my section was part of the material management section, the first to go. I advise you when working in corporate America, pay attention to who moves in and out of your department. If you start to see the token whites disappear, beware, there is something brewing that no one is talking about. Boeing was fair towards me in my departure; they paid a year's salary and a pension. Who could ask for more? I do fault J. D. for the demise of our department if he had only listened to reason. The material move started the distrust from upper management painting a dark cloud over everyone's head, thus, resulting in over 300 people being laid off.

A year has passed since working for Boeing, I have built a deck, planted a garden, went on a cruise, and picked up a new job at the Department of Veterans Affairs. It did not take long for me to get started. My boss was Nancy Duncan, the head of an agency contracted by the VA. Nancy hired me as a Material Manager in the supply and logistics department. This is where I saw the true colors of the VA; they do not have a great reception for Veterans. I feel that the VA despises Disabled Veterans who work there especially if one is not white. A position was coming up in the logistics department and I was the one most qualified for the position. I met all the prerequisites for the job but a white guy was chosen. He had zero logistics training and was placed to lead several people with extensive knowledge in the field. I asked about it and the white supervisor told me I was not right for the position which meant I was not the right color for the position.

I later applied for a contract specialist position and again I was denied. After the fifth denial, I questioned the human resources department about why I was not being selected; after all the denials, I was selected for a GS nine to thirteen position. However, to take the job, I would be required to downgrade from a GS-11 to a GS-9 with a pay grade increase every year until I reach the GS-13 level. Working in this field, I learned a lot about white corporate America. The smarter you are as a Black man, the harder it is to succeed. White men dominate the government contracting field. It does not matter how smart you are or how much education you have as a Black man If you are in a room of dumb white people. There were no Black people in my chain of command to the president and that was President Obama. The VA, in my opinion, does not like the Veterans they serve. As a Veteran, a Black man, and working for them, I experienced more than thirty (30) acts of discrimination. These people would not allow me to succeed as a Contract Specialist. But, as resilient as I am, I was still successful. Promoted as a Civil Servant from a GS-9 to GS-12 in three years and scheduled to receive GS-13 in the next twelve months. When the people in power realized I would be promoted, they started a strategy to keep me down. Mind you, up to this point, I have received nothing but marks of excellence on the six annual examinations. Once I realized this was the case, I filed an EEOC report and they accepted the case. Now the heat is up; white people will do anything to look innocent of a crime, despite the atrocities committed. I can never trust them anymore; not even the doctors, the lawyers, the police, not even the school teachers.

Some time ago, a charitable organization sponsored a free Friends and Family Day picnic from eleven until four o'clock. This picnic was to show appreciation for the groups of people who supported them throughout the year. Church groups and private organizations have been great supporters of non-profit organizations. One local church group had differences in opinion with the order in which they were serving the free meals. They complained because the homeless kids were served before them. The committee had made arrangements with the local groups and churches to perform different skits and acts at different times during the picnic. This particular church group had agreed to perform an act at one o'clock that afternoon. Unfortunately, the group had difficulty gathering members of the group so they were late arriving. They arrived at three-thirty that afternoon and immediately went to the stage to perform the act. Keep in mind that the picnic was free and all had been notified of the ending time. A special group was invited to the picnic; they were wards of the state and came from foster homes and state-run facilities. About twelve of these many kids from the Child Protective Services were allowed to make the trip to the picnic. The Forgotten Child Foundation made the arrangements and assumed responsibility for the twelve kids.

The picnic was truly an important outing for these kids. The Child Protective Service had a caseworker at the picnic to monitor their behavior because the kids are in protective custody. They arrived at the picnic around three after looking for the park for the last hour. The kitchen had set aside meals for these kids and when they arrived, we all helped out in getting them a meal. This was a wonderful sight to see them enjoy a nice BBQ meal; they kept coming back for more and we fed them. About the time of their arrival, several events were taking place. The kitchen was preparing to close; the "late" praise dancers were finishing their act. The committee knew that this event was coming to an end. They prepared the last plates for the crowd. The Praise team came to the serving window for food and it was all gone. Again, keep in mind a "free" picnic. The leader of the group immediately displayed unacceptable behavior. These church members and servants of God complained that we had given their food to the kids who were from the Child Protective Service. This was truly a bedrock display of a hypocritical character that was unworthy. The members of this praise team were all from affluent families and communities. To think that they were more important than the forgotten children is a contradiction of our belief system. The praise team is part of the "haves" in our society and they wanted to deprive the "have-nots".

FIRST BUSINESS

White men were still falling in love with a pretty Black woman back then, and still to this day. Muddear, my mother, was a very pretty woman; she was mean and all, but very pretty. I am glad she kept her distance from white men. Never can I recall a time where Muddear encountered a white man for anything. She did her domestic work but not for long, she got a job at the Care Inn in Indianola taking care of old white people. This was after she attended Mississippi Delta Junior College for a year to get her certification in Nursing Assistance. That job did not last long; they eventually accused her of stealing a freaking bag of oranges. She was fired after they did not believe she was innocent so she sued them. After about a year of back-and-forth litigation, she won a cash settlement and they offered her the job back, but she refused. Muddear took the settlement and opened a little café called "Cat's Place." I could be a little backward on my story. What made me back up is remembering the time I was on the bar on a pillow in a Chiquita banana box. I had to be less than a year old because I could not walk at the time. Seems like I was big enough to remember the things I saw. An old man was taking his time about leaving Cat's Place; by the time he made it to the door, it was too late. Muddear threw a glass ashtray that hit the wall next to the door shattering into a thousand pieces. The ashtray shattered against the wall barely missing the man's head. Needless to say, he hurried out of Cat's Place never looking back. Cat's place had a pinball machine, a pool table, a cigarette machine, and a few other amenities. Looking back at the place, it was a shack with a wooden floor and air. The room was a speakeasy in poor condition but the people never mind. It was somewhere to go after working on the plantation driving tractors. Muddear cooked hamburgers for sale back then and they were good sellers.

Don't confuse who I am with what you do; this [I am] is a state of being, not a behavior. I believe in righteousness for every person!

No man or woman was born with equality making us all live a different path. Every man and woman choose sometimes good and sometimes bad. Whatever the choice, we must live with it. So, our choices design our future. Words for the universe, happy Friday! No reason, just thinking out loud!

BIBLIOGRAPHY

Art T. Burton, *Bass Reeves, Deputy US Marshal: A Legendary Lawman on the Western Frontier Who Rode for Judge Isaac Parker.* Persimmon Hill (June 1992).

Art T. Burton, *Black, Red and Deadly: Black and Indian Gunfighters of the Indian Territory.* 1870–1907. Austin, Texas. Eakin Press, 1991.

Heim, Joe. *How a Long-Dead White Supremacist Still Threatens the Future of Virginia's Indian Tribe.* June 2015.

(Judge, Monique, 10/28/18, *Don Lemon: White Men Are the Biggest Terror Threat in This Country).* Don Lemon Declaration, Deerwester, Jayme. (11-1-2018). *USA Today Magazine*

Willie Lynch Speech of 1712. https://formspal.com/pdf-forms/willie-lynch-letter-the-making-of-a-slave/

C. Vann Woodward, "Plessy v. Ferguson: The Birth of Jim Crow," *American Heritage* (Volume 15, Issue 3: April 1964).

Urofsky, Melvin I. *The Affirmative Action Puzzle, A Living History from Reconstruction to Today.* 2020, 1st ed.

ABOUT THE AUTHOR

Warren Jay Smith Sr. was born in Inverness, Mississippi, on 31 July 1959, to George Reed, and Helen Smith. He received Christ at the age of six at New Hope M. B. Church located in Inverness. His other community activity includes the Cub Scout Pack, Boy Scouts Troop # 349 and a member of Inverness Elementary School marching band, as a baritone horn player. Prince Smith graduated from Gentry High School in Indianola, Mississippi in 1977.

He then enlisted in the United States Army. Prince Smith has served his country twenty-one consecutive years. During his tenure in the military, he earned the rank of Master Sergeant. Prince Smith received his associates' degree in technology from Pierce College in Tacoma, Washington, his Bachelor of Arts in Human Services from Wayland Baptist University and his Masters of Arts in Procurement and Acquisition Management from Webster University.

In 1986, Prince Smith was initiated into the Prince Hall Masonry in Lawton, Oklahoma by Mistletoe Lodge # 31. He is currently a member of Eureka Consistory #113 and he was the founding Commander in Chief of Booker T. Alexander Consistory # 117. Prince Smith was nominated and received his 33rd Masonic degree in 1997. Prince Smith is married to Dr. Jacquelyn E. Smith, an Associate Professor at Our Lady of the Lake University. Prince Smith has three biological children: Warren J. Smith II, Jacqua Jackson and Kayla M. Manja.

Prince Smith has also helped to foster the lives of his adopted children: Chanel Ki'shonna Smith, Andrea, Audrey and Alisha

Gray. His businesses included a lawn care company, a book store and a restaurant/bar. He intends to keep teaching, coaching and counseling our youth.

www.ingramcontent.com/pod-product-compliance
Lightning Source LLC
Chambersburg PA
CBHW051831160426
43209CB00006B/1127